"Susie Larson is the real deal. No pretense in this lady! You will laugh, cry, and sigh as she shares her joys, sorrows, and humiliations. Get ready to discover your buried passion. Be prepared to go deeper in intimacy with your Lord. This book will motivate and push you to grow! I highly recommend *Your Beautiful Purpose*!"

—Linda Dillow, author of *Calm My Anxious Heart*
and co-author of *Intimate Issues*

"This is a vulnerable book, an honest book, a beautiful book filled with hope and promise. God will meet you in these pages."

—John Eldredge, author of *Wild at Heart*,
Captivating, and *Beautiful Outlaw*

"Susie has such a beautiful way of making you feel at ease—in her conversations and in her written word. She spills grace as she welcomes you into her life and makes you feel like you've known her for years. I always look forward to talking with her and am honored to have my name appear on this beautiful work."

—Angie Smith, author and Women of Faith speaker

"For every woman who has ever wanted to dream big dreams for God, this book is for you! With wisdom and insight, Susie Larson points us to the humble boldness and Spirit-led passion we need to fulfill the beautiful purpose God has designed and assigned each one of us."

—Joanna Weaver, author of *Having a Mary Heart
in a Martha World*

"Susie writes with such tender honesty and compassion that you will connect to her immediately. Then she will take you to hidden truths of God that will convict, encourage, and equip you to walk in 'your beautiful purpose.' Not a word is wasted in this book—it's pure gold!"

—Dr. Juli Slattery, president/co-founder of Authentic Intimacy;
psychologist and author

"*Your Beautiful Purpose* is a transparent, practical, and timely book. Using examples from her own life, Susie has given women the real life tools they'll need to live fully aware of God's love while engaged in His purpose for their lives."

—Lisa Bevere, author and speaker;
co-founder of Messenger International

Books by Susie Larson

Blessings for the Evening
Blessings for the Morning
Your Beautiful Purpose
Your Sacred Yes

Your Beautiful
Purpose

Susie,

Let peace

rule & reign!

Susie

Your Beautiful
Purpose

Discovering and Enjoying What
God Can Do Through You

SUSIE LARSON

BETHANY HOUSE PUBLISHERS
a division of Baker Publishing Group
Minneapolis, Minnesota

© 2013 by Susie Larson

Published by Bethany House Publishers
11400 Hampshire Avenue South
Bloomington, Minnesota 55438
www.bethanyhouse.com

Bethany House Publishers is a division of
Baker Publishing Group, Grand Rapids, Michigan

Printed in the United States of America

Library of Congress Cataloging-in-Publication Data
Larson, Susie.
    Your beautiful purpose : discovering and enjoying what God can do through you / Susie Larson ; foreword by Ann Voskamp.
        p. cm.
    Includes bibliographical references.
    ISBN 978-0-7642-1066-2 (pbk. : alk. paper)
    1. Christian women—Religious life. I. Title.
BV4527.L377 2013
248.8′43—dc23   2012034647

A portion of chapter 3 is adapted from *Embracing Your Freedom* by Susie Larson (Chicago: Moody Publishers, 2009), 178–181, and is used by permission.

Unless otherwise indicated, Scripture quotations are from the Holy Bible, New International Version®. NIV®. Copyright © 1973, 1978, 1984, 2011 by Biblica, Inc.™ Used by permission of Zondervan. All rights reserved worldwide. www.zondervan.com Version

Scripture quotations identified ESV are from The Holy Bible, English Standard Version® (ESV®), copyright © 2001 by Crossway, a publishing ministry of Good News Publishers. Used by permission. All rights reserved. ESV Text Edition: 2007

Scripture quotations identified GW are from GOD'S WORD®. © 1995 God's Word to the Nations. Used by permission of Baker Publishing Group.

Scripture quotations identified HCSB are from the Holman Christian Standard Bible, copyright 1999, 2000, 2002, 2003 by Holman Bible Publishers. Used by permission.

Scripture quotations identified THE MESSAGE are from *The Message* by Eugene H. Peterson, copyright © 1993, 1994, 1995, 2000, 2001, 2002. Used by permission of NavPress Publishing Group. All rights reserved.

Scripture quotations identified NKJV are from the New King James Version. Copyright © 1982 by Thomas Nelson, Inc. Used by permission. All rights reserved.

Scripture quotations identified NLT are from the *Holy Bible*, New Living Translation, copyright © 1996, 2004, 2007 by Tyndale House Foundation. Used by permission of Tyndale House Publishers, Inc., Carol Stream, Illinois 60188. All rights reserved.

The Internet addresses, email addresses, and phone numbers in this book are accurate at the time of publication. They are provided as a resource. Baker Publishing Group does not endorse them or vouch for their content or permanence.

Cover design by Faceout Studio

Author is represented by The Steve Laube Agency

15 16 17 18 19 20 21   13 12 11 10 9 8 7

green press INITIATIVE

For My Dad
Who taught me how to fight.

For My Mom
Who taught me how to love.

For My Savior
Who taught me how to live.

Contents

Foreword

My chronic illness flares. I can't find my wallet. The kids are too loud—until glass shatters somewhere.

I catch my breath.

In the still, there's this hiss: "Now look what you did."

I don't want to know what just broke.

Because I know I am.

One morning in spring, I am shards on a floor and it's hard to breathe and I can't gather all the pieces and I don't know where peace is and how in the world I am going to piece together a beautiful purpose here when everything just keeps slipping through my fingers to break.

I have no words when a friend knocks on the front door and hands me a journal embossed with one simple word: *PEACE.*

How can she know?

I hold the journal with that one simple, frustratingly elusive word embossed across it—*PEACE*—and my chin drops to my chest and everything trembles and there's no holding on to my own breaking, everything giving away. Purpose. Peace. *Please.*

There are reasons why certain books find their way to your hands.

There are days when you are just desperate, just wild, just about at a breaking point—because until you understand your purpose, you'll overestimate your peace.

I go for walks down through the woods. Sit by the pond, pray, read Scripture. Write in that journal. Run my hands across that one word: Peace. Some days the angst tightened around my chest in a relentless grip as I walked home: *How can I be a more patient mother, a more loving wife, a more earnest disciple? How can I become all God needs me to become—before I can do what God called me to do? How can I abandon the pressures and abide in His promises?*

And how in the world do you move these things from what you know—to what you breathe?

I go away to a cottage for a few days, soak in the Psalms. Peace pools around my toes, wetting me, quenching me . . . and then ebbs away again, lost at sea as waves of worries flood in.

Peace may come fleetingly as a reviving, necessary place—but peace as a place, it's always like a fog burning off in the heat of the day; peace as a place will always dissipate.

Places come and go. Tickets are expensive and the cost of coffee adds up.

I come home to the noise, to the kids, to my mess, to me . . . and I read it right there in His Word. Lay my hand right across the verse like a finding, like a beginning again, like pure beauty— my treasure: "For he himself is our peace" (Ephesians 2:14).

And there is the crux of it—peace isn't ultimately a place. Peace is the ultimate Person.

And the Person of Christ has an ultimate purpose in Christ— *just for you.*

"*Listen carefully to what God the Lord is saying,* for he speaks peace to his faithful people" (Psalm 85:8 NLT), for the Lord of peace Himself gives us "*his peace* at *all* times and in *every* situation" (2 Thessalonians 3:16 NLT).

When I read these pages of Susie Larson's, when I read her stories and her startling wisdom and her fresh insights and of her tender walk with our Savior, I feel like someone has filled up all the pages of my Peace journal—that someone is showing me—*practically, page by page, purposefully*—how to go deeper with the Person of Christ, the purpose of my life, and the peace of my days.

There are few books that make you feel like you have just found a mentor, just found a sister—just found out how to hold on to everything that keeps slipping through your fingers.

It doesn't matter how chaotic your life is.

It doesn't matter how long you've been waiting, what your hope is, what your impossible prayers are.

It doesn't matter how broken you are.

The Prince of Peace is bent beside you right now—you holding this book, because He knows—and He's picking up all the pieces to your peace.

To make this mosaic of astonishing grace.

To piece you together for His one beautiful Purpose.

So turn the page . . . and breathe.

~Ann Voskamp
Bestselling author of *One Thousand Gifts*

Because we know that this extraordinary day is just ahead, we pray for you all the time—pray that our God will make you fit for what he's called you to be, pray that he'll fill your good ideas and acts of faith with his own energy so that it all amounts to something. If your life honors the name of Jesus, he will honor you. Grace is behind and through all of this, our God giving himself freely, the Master, Jesus Christ, giving himself freely.

2 Thessalonians 1:11–12 THE MESSAGE

It's time to begin the journey of your life. May your heart sing as you embrace everything God has planted there.[1]

—Bruce Wilkinson

Introduction

Do You Believe
You're Called?

God is in the process of educating us for future service and greater blessings. And if we have gained the qualities that make us ready for a throne, nothing will keep us from it once His timing is right.[1]

—L. B. Cowman

Beautiful: Magnificent, Stunning, Delightful, Divine, Winsome, Engaging, Appealing

Purpose: Aspiration, Plan, Conviction, Motivation, Resolve, Intention, Aim[2]

Bless you for picking up *Your Beautiful Purpose.* May God speak deeply to your heart and awaken fresh purpose in your soul as you read on.

In case you're wondering if this book is for you, know that I had three women in mind while working my way through these pages.

The first is the woman with a buried passion, a desire in her heart to be fulfilled. She lights up when she talks about what she'd so love to do someday. But it all seems so far off, so unattainable, that she wonders if she's delusional, or just dreaming.

If that's you, this book is for you. God has a plan and purpose for you that takes time to unfold, requires your cooperation, and goes beyond what your own mind can conceive. I pray you'll join me on this journey as God trains and readies you for your beautiful purpose.

I'm also thinking of the woman who's been so beat down by life, had so many of her heartfelt desires pushed aside, that she's barely alive, hardly passionate. The light's gone out of her eyes, life is mostly a duty, and she's quite sure it'll always be this way. She's afraid to dream because she'd rather not be disappointed.

If that's you, dear one, I wish I could wrap my arms around you. Please hear me when I say, this book is for you too. I prayed for you while writing this book. With all my heart I believe God wants to impart renewed hope and inspired vision to you. He wants to bring *life* back to your life. Join me on this journey and see if God won't breathe something fresh and beautiful into your soul.

Finally, I'm thinking of the woman who is earnest in her walk with Jesus but doesn't resonate with words like *dream* or *calling*. She just wants to be faithful right where she lives. She loves her familiar territory but lives unaware of the *more* God has for her. And what a beautiful soul she is! If that's you, I believe strongly that this book is for you as well. God wants to deepen your impact, stretch your faith, and widen your influence in a way that fits you perfectly. Will you join me on this journey? I pray you will.

The fact that you're standing here today with breath in your lungs testifies that God has a plan and purpose for you on this earth. Jesus wants you to live with bold confidence in His promises and humble dependence on His voice. He plans to transform you into a woman of purpose and lead you to places you could never otherwise go apart from Him.

What's so beautiful about our call is that God knows full well whom He's getting when He calls us.

In his book *Holy Ambition,* Chip Ingram reflects on the people God loves to use:

> God has chosen very regular, ordinary, common people just like you and me to accomplish the biggest events in all of human history. He used a teenage girl to bring His Son into this planet. He used a blue-collar worker to raise Him from childhood and teach Him about a life of integrity and worship. He used common fishermen to lay the foundation for the greatest revolution that has ever touched the world. And God wants to use you and God wants to use me in the same ways.[3]

God's will for you is your best-case scenario. I marvel at how He lovingly takes our broken pieces, our tangled-up fears, our worst mistakes, and creates a mosaic of beauty that impacts the world.

Consider the desires in your heart. Pay attention to stories that stir up your passions. Dare to believe that He wants to use the gifts He's imparted to you. He's the one who put desires *in you* that He might fulfill His purposes *for you.* He can even use the worst things you've ever done, or the worst things that have ever happened to you, to change the world through you. He desires to transform you into a humble, bold, healed, and confident woman who trusts Jesus with her every breath.

Join me as we awaken to the God-possibilities in our lives. I ask you to read through the chapters prayerfully and thoughtfully. May this be for you a life-transforming, soul-stirring journey. I pray it will be. As you work through the pages of the book you will learn to:

~ believe that God desires more for you than to just get by;

~ sort through the anxieties and insecurities that hold you back;

- put your fears under your feet and set your jealousies aside;
- dream with God about your beautiful life purpose;
- understand how God is using your current trials to train you for a greater purpose;
- silence the enemy's condemning voice and tune your ear to God's song over your life;
- lay hold of God's promises in a fresh, bold way; and
- walk forward in a new level of holy confidence and humble dependence.

A Life of Promise

So what kind of life did God promise us? Not an easy one. But a powerful, world-changing, redemptive, miraculous life that overcomes hardship, defies the odds, defeats the giants, and conquers fears.

If we take God at His word, He'll take us places and work through us in ways that will cause others *who knew us when,* to step back, shake their heads, and say, "There *has* to be a God in heaven; no way could she have accomplished those things or become that person on her own."

Jesus promised us an abundant life, which in essence involves copious amounts of fruitfulness, lavish amounts of love, abundant supplies of strength and courage, and profuse amounts of generosity. Jesus came to give us *life.* Satan came to steal it from us, to kill our dreams and our passion, and destroy every hint of God-inspired sparkle and verve within us (see John 10:10).

Jesus also promised that during our time on earth, we'd encounter hardship, trials, and tribulations (see John 16:33). We'll be misjudged, mistreated, and misunderstood. Satan will do everything he can to take us out. But here comes another promise: Overwhelming victory is ours in Christ Jesus (see Romans 8:37)!

Search the Scriptures yourself and you'll see verse after verse that speaks to our calling—our purpose—and of God's faithfulness to His promises. Perhaps the most compelling verse for me when it comes to our pre-ordained purpose on earth is Ephesians 2:10: "For we are God's masterpiece. He has created us anew in Christ Jesus, so we can do the good things he planned for us long ago" (NLT).

Do you actually believe that God wants to use you? That He has a beautiful assignment *just for you*? Are you ready to grab hold of God's promises right here, right now, no matter what your circumstances may be telling you? Will you dare to believe that God is working in you today to get you where you need to go tomorrow?

God is for you and loves the idea of using you for His great glory. You have a divine appointment to live an overabundant, more-than-fruitful life. Will you trust Him enough to look up and give Him your yes? I pray you will.

Jesus created you with a very specific purpose in mind. To live the powerful, significant life assigned to you by God, you must—with God at your side—confront the bullies of fear, insecurity, and inferiority. You must be gritty enough to walk by faith, be tenacious enough to grab hold of His promises and never let go, and be humble enough to admit that you need Him every single hour. He beckons you toward a battle, but you stand on the winning side.

Look for Him in your circumstances and you'll find Him there. May you dare to dream with God! You don't need to look to other women and long for their lives and callings. You don't need to be captivated by your fears.

No one and nothing can deter you from your calling—not your obstacles, not the woman you constantly compare yourself to, and not even your past sins and missteps. *Only unbelief* can keep you chained to mediocrity and a less-than life. Will you trust Jesus and begin to move forward in faith?

You have this one life to live. What will you do with what Christ has offered you? Will you spend your energy trying to present well, save face, and pretend you're not insecure? Or will you get real, face down your fears, and embrace the God-confident, significant life you were made for?

Do you know that the devil sees your potential with greater clarity than you do? That's why he works overtime to keep you from seeing who you really are in Christ. Lord willing, this book will teach you how to fight, how to stand, and how to move forward into the purposes God planned for you long ago. You'll learn how to trust God's timing and better discern His voice as you take each promised step on your journey.

May God open your eyes to all He has imparted to you! I dare you to dream with God and walk out His stunning purpose for you.

As a beautifully loved woman of God, you need only to look to Him who leads you joyfully with triumph.

May God bless you as you read
~Susie Larson

How to
Use This Book

Please use this book in a way that most suits you. If you grow best in the context of a women's Bible study group, approach this as a six-week study and complete two chapters each week. Do the Study Questions on your own and work through the Discussion Starters during your group time. Your group leader may want to delve deeper into the study questions during the group meeting.

Also available is a *DVD Study Companion*, which includes six thirty-minute segments that cover and expand on the material in this book, two chapters at a time. Together, the book and DVD set allows for study groups to host a six-week study at home or church.

A quick side note: Some of the Discussion Starters probe deeply and may feel too personal to address with others unless you're with your closest confidantes. You decide where you want to go with the Discussion Questions.

You may prefer to work your way through the book during your alone times with God and talk your way through it with a few close girlfriends.

Either way, I encourage you not to take this journey alone. Invite others to stand with you, pray with you, and spur you on as you consider God's beautiful purpose and plan for your life.

I ask you to dig into Scripture with a teachable heart and be fully present with God as you work through the Study Questions at the end of each chapter. Dare to take a few risks as you explore the Discussion Starters at the end of each chapter.

I want this book to feel like an encouraging note from a friend, inspiring you to be all you were meant to be in Christ Jesus. I believe in you. And more important, Christ Jesus loves you and believes you're worth His investment in you. God be with you as you dare to lay hold of His profound promises and His beautiful purpose for you.

Embrace Your Purpose

Take delight in the Lord,
and he will give you the
desires of your heart.

Psalm 37:4

Believe
You're Called

For we are God's masterpiece. He has created us anew in Christ Jesus, so we can do the good things he planned for us long ago.

Ephesians 2:10 NLT

God loves people. He is not that interested in our bigness, wealth, popularity, or supremacy. He is interested in our relationship with Him and our relationship with people.[1]

—Matthew Barnett

Have you ever noticed how faith steps can bring on a little nausea from time to time? Whether God asks me to share my faith with a stranger or do missionary work halfway around the world, those inner nudges make my stomach flip and my heartbeat quicken. Sometimes I fear I'll get it wrong, fall on my face, or misinterpret God's marching orders.

Even so, there's something else in me, something deeper, that loves to be challenged, loves the idea of stepping out in faith and seeing how God moves when I move with Him. I cherish that inner assurance and peace that often accompany God's call, a whispered voice that reminds me, *I'll miss out if I stay behind. My safest place is with Him, even if I don't know where He is taking me. I have to trust Him here.* Even when my offering isn't all I'd hoped it'd be, God moves on it, multiplies it, and changes me in the process. I marvel at how faithful God has been and how far He's brought me when I consider the person I was when He saved me.

When I was a young girl, my world turned upside down at the hands of a few teenage boys. Fear and insecurity became my new traveling companions. I didn't tell anyone what had happened until years later, long enough for the enemy's lies to get a good stranglehold on my sense of value and calling. My new sense of purpose as a young girl was twofold:

- To succeed at everything I attempted in order to prove to the world I wasn't the lost cause I believed myself to be.
- To control my environment so that I'd never be in a vulnerable situation again.

Jesus rescued my heart and saved my soul in eighth grade, but it would be many more years before I learned of His love in a way that compelled me to take risks, to trust Him, and to let down my guard.

Little by little, one step at a time, Jesus used the inner nudge to show me when to step out and when to step back. For instance, though I'd decided long ago that I would *never* take a mission trip (I'd pay for others to go, but I'd stay home), Jesus had decided long before that in due time, I'd trust Him enough to trample down my "nevers" and follow wherever He led me.

Before I learned—on a gut level—of God's unfathomable love and faithfulness, my sense of call revolved around my need for safety and control. It was my job to manage my fears and insecurities and somehow love Jesus from the smallness of my world. But eventually Jesus captured my heart and convinced me of His great love for me. And now I believe with all my heart that He is who He says He is. I know that where He guides, He provides. *He restored my soul, for His name's sake.*

If we trust God with our fears and insecurities, He'll entrust us with a call that puts those fears to shame. This faith walk is about intimacy with God. As we follow His lead, He'll lead us to rely on Him in ways big and small.

When God calls us out, whether it's to engage in a difficult conversation, to travel to a land far away, to reach out to a total stranger, or to attempt to accomplish something that's far bigger than we are, it can be both terrifying and exhilarating. When Jesus walked on the water in the fourth watch of the night, His disciples sat in the boat, terrified, believing Him to be a ghost (see Matthew 14:25–26).

I like to call these kinds of faith experiences God-opportunities. Oftentimes these ministry moments first appear to us as scary, risky, and inconvenient circumstances. If we cover our eyes and bury our head, we'll miss an opportunity to be part of an everyday miracle. Jesus calls us to faith and courage because He is faithful and strong. Read what He said to the disciples: "Take courage! It is I. Don't be afraid" (Matthew 14:27).

When a God-opportunity comes our way, He'll quicken our hearts, stir up our faith, and compel us to look past the fear. In essence, He says to us, "There's an opportunity here. Trust me. Take heart. And engage your faith. I control the storms and I have called you to this moment to see My glory and grow your faith."

Peter's response continues to speak to us today: "Lord, if it's you . . . *tell me to come* to you on the water" (Matthew 14:28, emphasis mine). What courage!

I think I have the spiritual gift of suspicion. The first time I read how Peter yelled to Jesus, *"If it's really You, Lord, tell me to step out of this boat and join You walking on top of the water"* (my paraphrase), I thought, *But, Peter, what if this really wasn't Jesus? The disciples thought Jesus was a ghost. What if it really would have been a ghost? What if the ghosts were all chuckling at each other, waiting and watching to see if you'd fall for their trick? It's like you set yourself up to sink! Aren't you afraid it's all a ruse?* And yet Peter knew his Shepherd's voice. And even more profound to me is this: *Peter asked to be called.*

In so many words, Peter said to Jesus, "Call me, Lord. I want to walk with You to unknown places. Wherever You are, I want to be there too. Through danger and storm and by still waters, I'll walk forward if You ask me to. I'll take the necessary risks required of me because I know You are with me."

Dr. Warren Wiersbe brings a profound insight to Peter's request:

> In fact, when Matthew wrote Peter's request, "Bid me to come," he used a Greek word that means "the command of a king." Peter knew that Jesus Christ was King over all nature, including the wind and the waves. His word is law and the elements must obey. . . . If Jesus says "Come" then that word is going to accomplish its intended purpose. Since He is the "author and finisher of our faith" (Hebrews 12:2), whatever He starts, He completes. We may fail along the way, but in the end, God will succeed.[2]

Dr. Wiersbe's insight compels me to make the same humble request to my King every single day: *Bid me come. Call me, Lord. Because I know if You call me, You'll sustain me.* Not only did Peter know his Savior's voice, Peter understood Christ's authority. Peter knew that if Jesus called him out, Jesus would also hold him up.

What Does It Mean to Be Called?

In technical terms, a calling is a vocation, a line of work. To get a spiritual perspective, let's look at the passage from Ephesians 2:10 again: "For we are God's masterpiece. He has created us anew in Christ Jesus, so we can do the good things he planned for us long ago" (NLT). God created us for Himself. He made us new in Christ Jesus so that we can do the wonderful things He planned for us. He created us with a purpose that He made provision for before we were born.

He had our lives and purposes on His mind before we even came to be. To use a double negative: You're not here for nothing! You're definitely on planet earth for a significant and important reason. From this point on, I'll refer to your purpose as your kingdom-call.

God assigns a certain sphere of influence and sends people our way to touch and love and influence. He even calls us to *become* a certain kind of person, one we could never be without God. As followers of Christ, we are ever and always *on-call* to represent Him to a lost and dying world.

Traveling around the country as a conference speaker, I meet far too many women who have a lifeless look in their eyes. They've stopped dreaming, or perhaps never dreamed at all. Either their fears have won the fight or their weariness has taken the fight right out of them. But when I push a little and ask a few provoking questions, I see the spark return. I know they have a deep desire to live the life God designed specifically for them. Life is too precious to live simply in reaction to our busy schedules or to our binding fears. We have work to do that will change us, fulfill us, stretch and beautify us. And through us, by the power of the Holy Spirit mightily at work within us, this work will change the world.

You and I have a calling on our lives. Scripture is clear. May God give you a strong sense of your kingdom-call so you can begin making life choices that line up with your divine and appointed purpose and direction.

Two Parts to Your Call

There's another aspect to our calling. And this part of the call is just as important, if not more so than the dream or vision we have for our lives. If we get so focused on our kingdom-call that we miss the daily call, we will be susceptible to selfish ambition, self-centeredness, and a self-important view of our role in God's kingdom work. And if we focus so much on the big-picture calling that we miss the importance of the present moment, we may get a wrong picture of what faithfulness (and even success) looks like.

Maybe you've seen it before. God inspires someone to start a ministry. Suddenly that ministry consumes its founder. She gives away all of her time, margin, and energy to her cause. She expects church leaders, friends, and neighbors all to care about the cause like she does. She feels worn out, frustrated, and a tad self-righteous. Without realizing it, she's forgotten that she only carries a portion of God's burden, while many others carry their portion of His heart for the world. Our lives are meant to intermingle with each other while tending to the tasks God gives us. Our kingdom-call matters, but we'll lose our way if we miss the other part of our call.

So what's more important than the overarching purpose written over our lives? It's the *daily* call to listen to God's voice and do what He says, to walk with *purpose in every step.* Moreover, if we tend to the daily call, if Jesus has our full attention from day to day, moment to moment, He'll get us where we need to go so that we can live out the big-picture, divinely appointed call written over our lives.

Oftentimes, those up-close acts of obedience seem completely unrelated to the overall direction of our kingdom-call. In fact, sometimes those little pit stops will seem to take us completely off track from our call. But Jesus knows what He's doing. The question is, do we love Him enough to trust Him?

Some days we'll be called to stop and help the person on the side of the road. Other days we'll be called to write a note to an old friend and apologize for letting too much time pass between visits. Some days Jesus will ask us to put more money in the offering plate and fewer items in the shopping cart.

There'll be whole seasons of life spent serving in ways that don't seem to match our gifts or passions, seasons where we feel overlooked and completely missed, seasons where the storms of life seem to focus their fury on us. But if God leads us to it, He'll lead us through it. And we can know that He has for us in that time and place, a very distinct purpose. And we must trust Him.

God calls us—above and beyond everything else—to live as ones who are spoken for. He knows where we should go and what we should do. We belong to Jesus, and it's our greatest privilege and responsibility as His followers to listen to His voice and do what He says. He knows how to get us where we need to go. And as I mentioned before, His will for us is our best-case scenario.

Keep Your Eyes on Jesus

Peter managed to bravely step out of the boat and onto the water. Pause for a moment and really let that in. Peter walked with Jesus *on the water*! The other disciples stayed back in the boat. If the boat had windows, I'm sure those guys would have pressed their faces against them and shouted, "Peter, go for it!" or, "No, don't do it! You're too old!" But then again, maybe not. Either way, Peter hoisted up his robe, stepped over the edge of the boat, splashed his feet in the water, and proceeded to walk. And he didn't sink. At least not at first.

But then the winds picked up. The waves raged and splashed up against his legs. Peter's hair whipped him in the face. He took his eyes off of Jesus. He looked at the waves and started to sink. He cried out and Jesus steadied Peter once again. Still out on the water, still amidst raging winds, right there in the middle of the storm, Jesus asked, "You of little faith . . . why did you doubt?" (Matthew 14:31).

In his New Testament commentary, Dr. Warren Wiersbe shares, "This word translated *doubt* carries the meaning of 'standing uncertainly at two ways.' Peter started out with great faith but ended up with little faith because he saw two ways instead of one."[3]

Peter saw two ways instead of one. He saw his way, which threatened total disaster, and he saw Jesus' way, which defied the laws of gravity. How many of us do the same? We see the logical solution, which is no solution at all, but forget that Jesus stands on the water, beckoning us away from our self-made decisions. Jesus' ways are so often counterintuitive. But at some point we have to decide to trust Him.

God Rescues Us From Ourselves

Peter saw two ways instead of one. How many times have I been in that same boat? How about you? In the early years of our marriage, buried under all kinds of medical debt, threatened with the loss of our home, Kevin and I saw two ways instead of one and we stopped tithing regularly. And we started to sink.

We cried out to Jesus and He steadied us. He confronted our fear and small faith. We looked to Him again as the One who promised to supply our needs. We asked forgiveness for our small faith and for our disobedience. We tithed again. We fixed our eyes on Jesus so much so that our double vision faded away. We now saw only one way. We decided to trust in the Lord with all our hearts and not to lean on our own understanding of this financial storm. We knew that if we acknowledged Him in all of our ways, He promised to make a straight path for us through the storm (see Proverbs 3:5–6).

When our double-mindedness became a single-minded obedience to a loving, living God, we learned beyond a shadow of doubt that our God *will* supply all of our needs according to His supply, not according to our lack (see Philippians 4:19). He called us in that storm to trust Him and do what He said. And He promised to hold us up so the waters would not sweep over us. And that's just what He did.

As we faithfully tithed, we found ourselves participating in God's supernatural supply. Our cereal seemed to last longer. Our juice didn't run out as fast either. And though our bills exceeded our income, we paid them every month. The math didn't work, but then again it's not supposed to. That's why God's economy trumps ours. He takes our little faith-filled offerings and multiplies them. It took us a long time to pay off that medical debt, yet God met our needs in a way we could not do for ourselves.

In due time we wanted to do more than tithe. We sowed more and more seeds into ministries that God called us to support. Our faith grew. Our compassion for God's work grew.

And you know what happened? We saw the enemy's plan for our finances *fall apart* as God established His plan through us. Kevin and I know that part of our calling as a married couple is to be hilarious givers. We're not there yet, but we're on our way. Several years ago we made a goal that in ten years, we wanted to be living on half of our income and giving the other half away to the poor. We're excited at the thought of it.

How do we keep our head above water when the storms rage and the winds blow and threaten to take us under? We keep our eyes on Jesus. We trust Him for His faithfulness and supernatural influence in our lives. We determine His way is the only way. And we trust that if we follow Him today, He'll get us where we need to be tomorrow.

Rooted, Grounded, and Called

Like a beautiful tree planted in fertile soil, your calling and mine are anchored in God Himself. Like branches that reach far and wide, our lives—anchored in Christ—are meant to touch many, to provide fruit for the hungry, shade for the weary, and stability for the lost. May we send our roots down deep into the Lord's marvelous love, and live lives that remind the world that our powerful and loving God is very much alive today.

> But blessed is the one who trusts in the Lord, whose confidence is in him. They will be like a tree planted by the water that sends out its roots by the stream. It does not fear when heat comes; its leaves are always green. It has no worries in a year of drought and never fails to bear fruit.
>
> Jeremiah 17:7–8

Precious Lord,

What an honor and privilege it is to be linked in fellowship with You! I want to live with an ear bent toward heaven. Give me eyes to see, ears to hear, and a heart to do Your will. Stir up in me a passion for Your assigned purposes for me. Help me to love what You love, hate what You hate, want what You want, do what You would do, and say what You would say. I don't want to throw away one minute of my life. Awaken me with fresh purpose and passion and give me an acute sense of Your voice from day to day. Here I am, Lord. Call me out of the boat so I can walk on water with You! Amen.

STUDY QUESTIONS

1. Prayerfully read Ephesians 2:10 and spend some time waiting on God. What are some of the purposes He has assigned to you?

2. Read Titus 2:11–14 and make note of the following points:

   a. The grace of God appeared through Jesus to take us off one path and put us on another. Describe both paths. Have you ever experienced those paths? When?

3. Read 1 John 4:16–19 and answer the following questions:

   a. How does your life reveal that you "know and rely on the love God has for you"? (Give some specific examples.)

   b. How will growing now in the knowledge of God's love for us give us confidence on the day of judgment?

   c. How has God's love for you impacted your fears? (And conversely, how have your fears impacted your perception of God?)

4. We are under the Lord's care and under His charge. He'll provide for and protect us, but He also calls us. Read Isaiah 43:1–3 and 10–13, and take some time to write about how God promises to come through for you. Also, based on this passage, write down what He's asking of you today in this moment.

5. Read Proverbs 3:3–10 and list the promises side by side with the call to obedience (e.g., Trust, Lean Not, Acknowledge Him = Straight Paths).

6. As you look again at your list from question number five, which call to obedience most stands out to you (which call to obedience is God most speaking to you about)?

7. Write out a prayer asking God to give you more faith to trust and obey Him in those specific areas.

DISCUSSION STARTERS

1. What do you sense is God's call on your life?

2. In what ways has God worked in past experiences to shape your God-given dreams and desires? Who inspires you to live out your God-given call and why?

3. What obstacles are in your path right now?

4. What do you sense God saying to you in this particular season of life (as it relates to your call)?

5. What are some next steps He's asking you to make?

2

Love
Your Story

For jealousy and selfishness are not God's kind of wisdom. Such things are earthly, unspiritual, and demonic. For wherever there is jealousy and selfish ambition, there you will find disorder and evil of every kind.

James 3:15–16 NLT

Envy slays itself by its own arrows.[1]

—Greek Proverb

Many years ago, an out-of-the-blue bout of jealousy blindsided me. At the time, I had been walking closely with the Lord and felt mostly on track with God's direction and purpose in my life. Many years prior, when the Lord spoke strongly to my heart about writing and speaking, I began making choices that lined up with that call. Over time I saw God arrange circumstances, move obstacles, open doors, and change the season so I could walk out the next phase of His plans for me.

I loved my life and felt mostly fulfilled with my God-assignments (something I'd only dreamed of for years). In fact, my spilling-over plate put a spring in my step. The rhythm of my days allowed for rich devotional time in the morning, hard yet significant and purposeful work during the day, family time in the evening, and pillow time by 9:30 or 10:00. Throw in a few workouts each week and you had a giddy girl. Content and consistently stretched in my faith, I hadn't felt jealous of anyone for a very long time.

Then one day I met a darling, successful author/speaker friend. She was witty, confident, and did I mention successful? Her massive speaking events made mine look like small-group gatherings or backyard barbeques. My book sales compared to hers, well, never mind.

Her kingdom contribution, no matter how you sliced it, reached farther and had more impact than mine. And to top off this recipe for jealousy, she garnered lots of help, had lots of volunteers, and *made it all look easy*. As soon as I noted the contrast between her impact and mine (and of her apparent energy and my very real fatigue), I felt that familiar fist in my gut. I'd been down jealousy's road before. Way down. So far down the road that I lost sight of everything good in my life. Thankfully, years ago, through much hardship and humbling, the Lord taught me a valuable lesson in gratitude.

Whenever I looked from the left to the right comparing others' haves with my have-nots, I became the poorest woman on the planet. But when I chose to look upon the One who gave me life and breath and every promise with a yes, I quickly became the richest woman on the planet. Isn't it something how when we look His way, He changes us?

Those who look to Him are radiant; their faces are never covered with shame.

Psalm 34:5

For all the promises of God in Him are Yes, and in Him Amen,
to the glory of God through us.

2 Corinthians 1:20 NKJV

If we want to grow and mature and be happy, we have to
practice giving thanks, even when we don't feel like it. I learned
this lesson time and time again, each time with a deeper appreciation of God's patience with me in spite of my often ignorant
sense of entitlement.

Gratefulness is a sacred exercise. The devil cannot stand it
when all focus is on God and a soul looks up in praise. Scary
thing is, we let go of a grateful heart and of the idea that God is
wisely good when we compare ourselves with another. I thought
I had learned this lesson well—that gratitude and faith are the
antidote for envy. So how come that wretched jealousy parasite
almost took over my insides once again?

Here's the answer: Envy is a powerful motivator, and the
devil knows it. If he can get us to compare ourselves to another,
he can derail us—at least for the moment—from God's best
plan for us. There's nothing new under the sun. If he found an
opening for envy and jealousy before, he'll look for one again,
when we least expect it.

We gain nothing by committing the sin of comparison. In
fact, it only bears two kinds of fruit—pride or despair—neither
of which come from the Vine. If our comparisons put us on top,
we start to think we're something apart from God; if we find
ourselves on the bottom, we're tempted to think we're nothing
in spite of God. Notice how both make us look away from God.

I featured Ann Voskamp on my radio show several months
ago. She expressed this profound thought from her bestselling
book, *One Thousand Gifts*: "How we behold determines if we
hold joy. Behold glory and be held by God."[2]

Think about that again for a moment: *How* we behold determines *if* we hold joy. How do we anchor ourselves in Christ

amidst the strong currents of selfishness, envy, and pride? We trust God with our story. We embrace a heart of thanks and faith by looking for Him in every nook and cranny of life. And we refuse to be petty in spite of all the opportunities to do so.

A friend once challenged Ann to find and write down one thousand reasons to give thanks to God. From the stars in the sky to muddy footprints on the floor, Ann's eyes opened to the countless blessings around her. Ann saw Jesus in the small up-close places of life. For the first time in a long time she felt present, in the moment, with Jesus and with the thousands of gifts that surrounded her. She realized that her thousand reasons for giving thanks to God were actually a thousand examples of God's great love for her.

I decided to take Ann's challenge and write down a thousand gifts from God. My list started out easy:

- *Access to God's presence*
- *The love of Jesus*
- *The comfort and guidance of the Holy Spirit*
- *Morning's new mercies*
- *My husband*
- *My sons and daughters-in-law*
- *My pit bull, Memphis*

Once I listed all of my obvious and most important treasures, I found I had to look a little harder, search a little deeper. I awakened to the reality that God's goodness to me goes far beyond what my can eyes see simply by skimming life's surface:

- *New branches on an old tree*
- *The ever-changing sky*
- *The "I love you" hug after an argument*
- *Staying power*

This new challenge stirred up an old lesson that needs to stay with all of us if we want to last long and finish strong: We are never more fully alive than when we consistently *give* thanks to One who gives and gives and gives again.

Here's another quote from Ann's book: "This practice of giving thanks . . . this is the way we practice the presence of God, stay present to His presence, and it is always a practice of the eyes. We don't have to change what we see. Only the way we see."[3]

~

When I was tempted years ago to be jealous of my dear sister in Christ, the devil spewed ugly questions and comments at me: *Why aren't you selling books like she is? What's wrong with you? She's a five-talent girl, and you're a two-talent girl. You'll never be anything more than average. You'll never fully measure up. Never be successful. You'll always and only be a just-get-by girl.* The enemy's taunts took the wind right out of my sails and made my whole body ache.

Thankfully, the Lord spoke these profound words across my heart:

> *Do not go there! Back up. You are at a fork in the road and if you open yourself up to envy, you will go the wrong way! Jealousy is the enemy's bait to lead you to a dead end where you'll lose sight of everything I've taught you. Step back from here and embrace a greater perspective.*

> *The reason something stirred within you when you saw this woman is because she possesses something of your inheritance. She has something that I want to give you! Can you see it? Can you embrace the gift I've put in her? I'm about to lead you to a more spacious place. I'm about to get you more help. But first I have this question for you: Can you honor the "Me" in her? How you steward what you see in others will determine how much I can entrust to you.*

There are two questions you must answer before moving from this place: What will you do with what I have offered you? And what will you do with what I have offered others? As the Scripture says, jealousy and envy are demonic; they are open doors to every other kind of evil. Do not be sympathetic to the smallest hint of jealousy or envy in your soul! Rise up from this place, lift your chin, and pray blessings and protection on your sister. You don't know what her call requires of her. If you are faithful with her gifts, her fruit will be your fruit; her victory, your victory; and a great blessing will follow. Rise up O woman of faith and be faith-full! I have wonderful intentions of using you! Choose life! Choose to trust me! Be a gracious, noble woman. And whenever those winds of jealousy and envy start to blow, step back and look up. You'll see something of a promise before you. Lay hold of the promise and refuse the enemy's bait. There's no life in the low road. Trust me.

You don't hear too many sermons preached on the idea that jealousy and envy are demonic influences from the pit of hell, but they are. Like a loaded gun in the hands of a fool, envy and jealousy are dangerous tools in the enemy's hands intended to steal, kill, and destroy. (I hope this goes without saying, but this does not mean that if you see a woman with a red Corvette and you feel jealous, it's because God wants you to have a similar car!)

If we open our hands and hearts to envy and jealousy, the devil grabs the opportunity to tie up our hopes and dreams and choke the life right out of them. The love of God ceases to operate through us when envy has its way in us. Think about that for a moment. Instead of moving forward with faith-filled words and actions, we surrender ground in unbelief. When we choose envy or jealousy, we forsake the idea that God is good and knows what's best for us. Living out of a lie is no small matter.

Think of how different our lives would be if we refused the enemy's invitation to be jealous and envious of another woman.

God has a promise in this place for us! Imagine not only steward-ing well the gifts you see in others, but also walking in a whole new level of faith and expectancy! God has a desire for us here, but remember, so does the devil. Someone once said that both God and the devil have a plan for our lives. And we are the ones who cast the deciding vote.

We are all different, but the enemy's tactics are the same. What stirs up a little jealousy in you may not do the same for me. We have different bents, different desires. When you and I walk closely with the Lord, our desires become purer, our goals clearer. When faced with the opportunity to be jealous or envious, we can step back and see things from God's perspec-tive. Even though the devil wants us to fixate on what we we're missing out on, God wants our hearts to open up and see all of the blessings we do enjoy and all we've yet to possess in Him.

This insight has changed my life. Now when I see a woman I admire, I immediately pray for her protection and blessing. I pray, *Lord, bless my dear sister in Christ. Move and advance Your kingdom through her! Protect her from the schemes of the enemy. Keep her far from accusing tongues. Surround her with God-fearing leaders and protect her in her vulnerable moments. May we, Your servants, serve You well, advance Your purposes, and thwart the enemy's plan on the earth!*

When I pray this way, I sense God's *Yes!* in my soul, en-couraging me onward. This prayer of faithfulness shuts down the enemy's taunts and engages me in a kingdom-cause that is bigger than I am. Plus, when I pray from heaven's perspective, I steward and care for the gifts of another in the same way that I want someone to care for and cover me.

We cannot comprehend the kingdom power we activate when we pray for a co-laborer in Christ, especially one we're tempted to be jealous of. After I've interceded for my sister and fellow servant, I then ask God, *Is there something You've given her that You also want to impart to me?* And then I listen for a while.

You can't imagine the kind of hope and faith this inspires! I can think of one woman I regularly pray for because she possesses something that makes me stand up and pay attention. She oozes the love of God and the power of the gospel like not too many other women I have met; and I love that about her. The kingdom of God advances daily because of her.

Nothing in me is jealous of her, but do you think I want what she has? You bet I do! I pray for her as my co-laborer in Christ, and then I look to God that I might lay hold of that very kingdom conviction for which Christ has also apprehended me. It's no exaggeration to say that she is stunned and amazed at what God has done through her. All of the credit and glory goes to Him. I celebrate with her in my prayers and then I look up and pray, *Lord, I honor this woman. I love what You're doing through her. And I'll have what she's having. I want to make a God-sized difference in my world in a way that matches Your call for me!* I'm happy for her. Expectant for me.

Do you think this a selfish thing to do? If He pours more of His virtue and influence and impact into my life, does it mean He has less for you? Ours is a God of limitless supply! And since we please Him with our faith and it's to the Father's great glory that we bear much fruit, I'm going to ask, seek, knock, and believe that God wants more and more territory in my life that He may advance His purposes on the earth. And I challenge you to do the same.

The Bible says the pure in heart see God (see Matthew 5:8). When I fling aside the pettiness and the surface stuff that most women are quick to notice about each other, and instead I *look for* the Jesus in you, God opens my Spirit-eyes. When I embrace you as one of His own, He gives me the capacity to see the hidden treasures within you. With a pure heart, He lets me grasp the value of what He's doing in you. In that process I'm made rich by all the beauty flowing out of your life. Love nourishes us. Jealousy starves us.

How do we overcome jealousy and envy and come to a place where we can embrace our story? We bow down and ask forgiveness for the absence of a grateful heart. We repent of, renounce, and reject any sense of entitlement or ingratitude. Then we raise our hands to God in praise. We count our blessings out loud, and by faith we thank Him for the blessings that *are on their way.* We pray for our co-laborers in Christ and sincerely lift our own hopes and dreams to the One who loves us.

We trust anew that He has a beautiful plan for us, one that we'll absolutely love if we'll only trust Him. With a renewed heart we receive a fresh dose of hope for our future and grace in our perspective. We refuse to act on or speak from a jealous mind-set. As Scripture says, we put to death the deeds of the flesh. We give no room for them to grow in our lives. If we want to possess everything God has for us, we must refuse any counterfeit the enemy sends our way.

When we walk through painful, trying, and testing seasons and we notice other women who seem blessed and light-footed as they flit from day to day, it's tempting to want to throw our book, our story, across the room and imagine ourselves in another's story. But we must not give up simply because we're walking through a difficult chapter in life. If we stay the course with Jesus, we're going to love how it all turns out. When it's all said and done and we look back over our shoulder, we'll be glad we cherished our story, for it's the one that fits us best.

We are in this together. We're all in different stages and phases of growth and development, but we're all precious to God, all a work in progress, all engaged in the priceless work of the kingdom. Do remember that what we *notice* in others is something that we already possess to some degree—or at least have the potential to—both positively and negatively. When we refuse the weakness and pettiness of a jealous spirit and instead rise up as co-laborers tending to a greater cause than our momentary selfish whims, the enemy is the one who gets blindsided. When we're together—refusing to let pettiness divide—he cannot tell where you end and I begin. All he can see is an unbeatable army.

> We are intimately linked in this harvest work. Anyone who accepts what you do, accepts me, the One who sent you. Anyone who accepts what I do accepts my Father, who sent me. Accepting a messenger of God is as good as being God's messenger. Accepting someone's help is as good as giving someone help. This is a large work I've called you into, but don't be overwhelmed by it. It's best to start small.
>
> Matthew 10:40–41 THE MESSAGE

Precious Lord,

Thank you for loving me like You do! I trust You with my today and with my tomorrow. Forgive me for so quickly going to jealousy when You always have a better plan and a better path for me. Help me to step back and look up when I'm faced with the temptation to be jealous or envious. I know You have a promise for me at every turn, and Your plan for me fits me perfectly. I will look for You in every nook and cranny of life. Help me to count my blessings and to embrace faith that You are not finished with me yet! I will follow You forever. Amen.

STUDY QUESTIONS

1. Prayerfully read James 3:15–16 and consider how often your thoughts—just this week—went toward jealousy and selfishness. Based on the passage you just read, notice how these wicked stepsisters open a door to every other kind of evil influence. Write down a prayer of repentance and reclaim your identity in Christ.

2. Now read James 3:17 and meditate on the idea that the wisdom we receive from above is both pure and loving. Spend a few moments praying for those you've struggled with this week. Bless those you're jealous of. And now write out a prayer of thanks for the story God is writing with your life.

3. Read Matthew 5:8 and spend some time here. We all struggle to view certain people with a pure heart, but it's our loss if we miss the blessing in them. To have a pure heart toward someone is to possess an uncontaminated, unmixed view of him or her. Ask God to see those specific few the way He sees them. Looking back over the past several years, how have you changed (grown) when it comes to viewing others with a pure heart? How have these perspectives impacted your thought life?

4. Read Psalm 106:24–25: "The people refused to enter the pleasant land, for they wouldn't believe his promise to care for them. Instead, they grumbled in their tents and refused to obey the Lord" (NLT).

   a. Put yourself in the shoes of a wilderness-walking Israelite. Has God put a promise in your heart that you've given up on? Have you begun to despise the dream in your heart? What kinds of words come out of your mouth regarding this situation? Write a prayer recommitting yourself to God's highest and best plan for your life.

5. Read Proverbs 14:30 and answer the following questions:

   a. In what areas of your life is your heart at peace? Explain why.

   b. In what ways do you struggle with insecurity, envy, and jealousy?

   c. Spend a moment with the Lord and let Him speak to you about those areas in your life. Ask Him to reveal the lie and to replace it with the truth. What truth is He speaking to you about today?

6. Why do you suppose a *heart at peace gives life to the body*? Describe how a peaceful heart might impact your life.

7. What steps do you need to take in order to cultivate a life that's more consistently marked by the peace of God?

DISCUSSION STARTERS

1. Do you know another woman who lives mostly unfettered by jealousy and envy? How does her life seem different from most?

2. Why do we as women perpetually deal with insecurity, and what can we do to walk more confidently, more consistently?

3. In what setting do you feel most secure, most accepted, most free to be yourself? Why do you suppose that is?

4. What has God taught you about your identity in Him? What do you do to hold on to that truth?

5. Do you have a dream hidden in your heart? Do you have a sense of your God-given purpose in this life? What is it?

Trust God's Timing

Trust God from the bottom of
your heart; don't try to figure out
everything on your own. Listen for
God's voice in everything you do,
everywhere you go; he's the one
who will keep you on track.

Proverbs 3:5–6 THE MESSAGE

Wait
on God

God has had it with the proud, but takes delight in just plain people. So be content with who you are, and don't put on airs. God's strong hand is on you; he'll promote you at the right time. Live carefree before God; he is most careful with you.

1 Peter 5:5–7 THE MESSAGE

We will only wait on Him with joy if we have deep confidence in His love for us.[1]

—David Timms

Years ago I went through a major refining period in my life (one of several). With my dreams on hold and my character flaws ever before me, God brought me through a time of painful yet necessary cleansing. I felt like a sailor, created to sail the open seas. And yet, for a season, God confined me to the beach to pick up garbage the tide washed in. Day in and day out I walked the shores, picked up the garbage, and watched as the other ocean-lovers sailed gleefully off to sea.

I knew I had the option to quit looking at my personal garbage and abandon this whole character-cleansing process. If I wanted, I could go make something happen on my own. I had a free will. But I wanted God's best for me. I wanted the fruit from my life to nourish people long after I passed into eternity. And more than anything, I wanted to be more like Jesus.

The Lord tested my resolve one day when I saw my dreams on someone else's sail. God had me in a hidden season, serving in youth ministry, which landed about number four or five in my gift-set. I love teens so very much, but I strongly felt called to minister to women. Yet God had me right where He wanted me—in a stretching, humbling, learning-how-to-obey-even-when-it-doesn't-suit-you mode. I really wanted to be a writer. Actually, I felt called to both a speaking and writing ministry. I'd been a speaker for a number of years, but even that ministry sat on the altar.

God led me away from my calling to a place of submission and obedience. I served on a leadership team in my very small church—a heavy, hidden mantle that called for thick skin and a tender heart. My husband and I also served countless hours as volunteer youth pastors. While these seasons bore fruit, they also revealed glaring weaknesses in me like fear, anxiety, insecurity, ambition, and impatience. The runaway bride in me longed to cut and run and get out of the house of mirrors, but God wouldn't release me from my duties. Besides, anywhere I'd try to run, there I'd find myself.

God's call to serve in a small church (when I longed to hide in a big church) built a hedge around my life and closed me off from my dreams. I didn't want to face the sins and weaknesses embedded in my soul, but God loved me too much to leave them there. In this place of loneliness, delay, learned obedience, and not-yets, the Lord taught me about purity of heart, kingdom motivation, and serving with excellence and a good attitude. I learned to thrive there. I learned to trust God in that place. But God sees things in us we don't even know are there. Apparently, more of "me" still had to go before He could take me to the next place.

There I served, all settled into my refining season, minding my own business, when a woman approached me and told me about all of the wonderful things going on in her ministry. Her speaking events took her all over the world, and she couldn't keep up with all of the requests. On top of that, someone approached her about writing a book. Surprised and excited, she blurted out, "I've never even *thought* of writing a book, and just like that, they asked me to write a book! What are the chances?"

I smiled at her and died inside. My dreams flapped on her sail, right in my face. The wind on her back messed up my hair. Her good news defeated me. I offered a weak smile and wished her the best. *Lord, forgive me for my selfish heart.*

The next morning during my prayer time, I sat down and apologized to the Lord for my attitude. I hugged my coffee cup and bowed my head to pray. *Lord God, I'm thoroughly ashamed of myself. Please forgive me for such a selfish response to her good news. It's no wonder You have me in this place of learning and refining. There seems to be no end to my selfishness. Please forgive me once again and make me more like You. I trust You, Lord. Have Your way in me. Amen.*

I surrendered my will and my dreams once again. I trusted Him to forgive me and to renew my resolve to obey Him amidst a time that wasn't easy or fun. God seemed silent, but I sensed His nearness. After a sacred, silent moment, He spoke to my heart. And His response to my prayer about knocked me over:

If the closest you ever get to a speaking and writing ministry is simply to pray for the success of that woman, will you do that for Me? Do you love Me enough to serve Me in this capacity: to humble yourself before Me by being her behind-the-scenes prayer support, even if she never knows it?

I did *not* see that coming. I couldn't even answer right away. I crawled down to the floor, put my face to the ground, took a deep breath, and prayed, "Um, I'm going to have to get back to you on that one."

I didn't have an honest yes in me at that moment. Sure, I'd pray for her, but I wanted to pray for me too. I so strongly sensed that God had called me to write and speak. I had dreams and passions and a message to share. And the thought of it all coming to nothing broke my heart. For three days I wrestled with my will, my hopes, and my selfish ambitions.

Finally, on the third day, I knelt down before the Lord. I put my head to the floor, and I said, "Yes, Lord. I will do that. You have me. All of me. I don't want one thing that You don't want for me. Besides, it doesn't matter what I do for You, if it's done out of a heart to honor me. This cannot be about my ambitions and goals; it's about Your kingdom work and getting it done in the best way possible. I am Yours. Do with me what You will." I meant every word.

I lifted my head and God flooded me with peace and an overwhelming sense of His presence. I loved Him more at that moment than I had in a long time. I kept my word, and for a season I prayed for the woman with the wind. After a while, God released me from the burden to intercede for her. I'd try to pray for her and it just didn't feel natural anymore. He gave me permission to move on.

The Bible says that pride goes before a fall and humility precedes honor (see Proverbs 29:23). Though refining times are difficult, God uses them for our protection. When we honor the Lord in the refining process, He lifts us up and blesses us before a watching world. Our honor isn't the goal, but He honors us just the same.

When life heats up, we have the choice to jump out of the refiner's fire with our pride still intact. But here's what's scary about choosing that route: the pride that helps us save face will eventually be the stumbling block that makes us fall on our face.

But when we humbly bow our face before the Lord, God considers it a great *honor* to reside in that humble place with us. Honestly, it's unfathomable that God allows us to carry things so dear to Him—His glory, His power, His Holy Spirit, His message to a lost and dying world—knowing that we will at times make mistakes, do it wrong, take the credit, and even completely miss the mark on occasion. He uses us on a Monday knowing we'll blow it on Tuesday. He knows how imperfect and self-centered we can be and yet He entrusts the greatness of heaven to His beloved ones.

Like a grandma who allows her small grandchild to carry the family heirloom, the Lord places in our hands a measure of His glory along with a God-sized calling. He surrounds us with grace and mercy and all of the supernatural help we could ever need. And then He leads us on and allows us to join Him in this kingdom work. What an absolute honor, wouldn't you say?

And then . . . He rewards *us* for having the faith and the courage to step up and work alongside Him! He knows how transient we are and yet He makes our heart His home. Amazing love.[2]

God revealed His wisdom and love by taking me through that refining process. Interestingly, the part of my call I most enjoy today, the area of service that's most instinctive to me, is radio.

My call is threefold: speaking, writing, and radio. And wouldn't you know I am most fulfilled when I am behind the microphone, promoting other authors, speakers, artists, and folks in ministry? I find my greatest delight in mining the treasures God has put inside others. I love the creative process of unearthing the spiritual truths from my guests in a way that encourages them and nourishes and strengthens the audience.

I shudder to think of what I would have missed out on had I not humbled myself before God and entrusted my whole self to Him. His ways are not our ways. His thoughts are far better than our thoughts.

It's Time to Wake Up!

Living numb is almost easier than waking up to a heartfelt dream or desire. When we're numb, we don't really know what we're missing. And we don't much care. But when we start to feel again, it's uncomfortable. When my foot falls asleep, it's useless for its intended purpose, but at least it doesn't hurt. Yet when I start to move again, the tingles and prickles make me want to smack my foot against the wall.

I've met countless women who live numb, and though they don't like it much, they prefer it to that uncomfortable process of waking up. Who wants to feel the prickled push to move from a safe but lifeless hideout?

Who wants to wrap hopeful fingers around a dream that we're not even sure belongs to us? The sting of such potential disappointment is enough incentive for long naps. Or numbness. But choosing the risk of waking up to our heart's desires is an important part of the process.

We cannot respond to Jesus' invitation to live significant lives for Him without coming alive in ways that surprise us. And as we come alive, we come undone—a feeling that's both unsettling and beautiful. From the time we wake up to God's divine purposes to the time we walk out those purposes in obedience and faith, we stand as works in progress, tested through trial, completed through perseverance. It takes guts to reach out a hand for Jesus and to follow Him to places unknown. Oftentimes, those places require humble surrender, gritty faith, and patient trust.

I'm mentoring a young mom whose beautiful purpose involves changing the foster care system. In fact, I use the term *mentoring* loosely because she inspires *me* every single time we talk. Jami and her husband, Clint, have two biological children and one adopted son.

Even with three children, this precious couple felt the call and the desire to adopt more children. And though they felt convinced that God put this desire in their hearts, they dealt with one disappointing hurry-up-and-wait scenario after another. Each time they seemed days away from holding their next adopted child, for one reason or another, those plans fell apart.

Jami cried out to God, so confused as to why God put this desire in her heart only to allow their plans to fall apart again and again. Then one day the Lord spoke these words to her broken heart: *This is not about you. It's not about bringing a child into your family. It's about bringing your family to a child.*

Jami and Clint learned about the half a million children currently in the foster care system, and God stirred in their hearts. They took the first steps to become foster parents. During that process they learned of the vast need within the system. While preparing to become foster parents, Jami and Clint organized a group of volunteers to paint and furnish their local county office.

That one magnificent act of service blossomed into a non-profit ministry. They founded The Forgotten Initiative, a national organization that reaches out to foster children, foster parents, and the foster system with help, encouragement, and support.

Jami and Clint also took in three more foster children, whom they eventually adopted. With six kids and a bursting-at-the-seams ministry, Jami is running to keep up with God and marveling every step of the way.

⁓

Waking up the sleeping and numb areas in our lives is God's work; we walk with Him, He awakens us. But then it's our turn to respond to Him. Once we see that Jesus indeed has a dream for us and that He fully intends to walk with us and fulfill His promises, we start to feel something come alive within us. We get excited. We find a yes in our souls and we lace up our shoes for the journey ahead.

And at exactly that moment, He asks us to slow down, to wait, and to trust Him as things crawl along at a snail's pace. Like my friend Jami, we wonder why God put a desire in our hearts only to delay its fulfillment.

When we've got fuel to burn and the passion bursting inside us, waiting, training, refining, and discipline all seem like huge wastes of precious time. Movement wakes us up, right? So why all of the sudden has God slowed down the process? This is an important question, one we must not pass over too quickly.

And the thing is, we do have a free will. We are free to run ahead, to manipulate opportunities, and to make things happen on a more efficient timeline if we wish to go that route. But God's process dwarfs ours every day of the week. It takes maturity and humility to first awaken to God's desire and then to humbly await His timing. But this wise and perfect training process strengthens and prepares us to last long and finish strong.

He Works for Those Who Wait for Him

We may go into the waiting times kicking and screaming, "Lord, I trusted You! You gave me a dream; I stepped out, and for what? Nothing's happening! I feel like a fool." But if you trust Him, you'll come out of this season leaning on the arm of your Beloved. "Lord, I trusted You and found You trustworthy. I now know that when You ask me to wait it's because You're making me ready. You had to remove from me the very things the enemy would have used against me. Your ways are always motivated by love. I embrace contentment because You are always my safest place. My refuge."

When the dream of service seems far off and our flaws and foibles cloud our view, it's the perfect time to be still and know that He is God (see Psalm 46:10). God knows how to speak to us in a way we'll understand. He knows what's in us that will hurt us later if we're not rid of it. He's so protective of us, so loving toward us that He'll never send us out unprepared.

The process of preparation can seem agonizingly slow at times. And yet He is intimately engaged with us in every detail and every minute of our journey. Over time I learned to pray this simple prayer: *Lord, I trust You in this place. If You make me wait, it's because You're making me ready. You give Your best gifts to those who trust in and wait on You. Amen.*

I love this insight from one of my favorite devotionals, *Streams in the Desert:*

> Waiting is much more difficult than walking, for waiting requires patience, and patience is a rare virtue. We enjoy knowing that God builds hedges around His people, when we look at the hedge from the aspect of protection. But when we see it growing higher and higher until we can no longer see over it, we wonder if we will ever get out of our little sphere of influence and service where we feel trapped. Sometimes it is hard for us to understand why we do not have a larger area of service, and it becomes difficult for us to "brighten the corner" where we are. But God has a purpose in all of His delays. "The steps of a good man are ordered by the Lord." (KJV)[3]

If you are in a waiting, not-yet season, slow down and let the Lord speak to you in this place. And when He does speak, do not harden your heart. When He addresses a weakness in your life, don't shrug it off like it's nothing, because it's something. And when He points out an area of inconsistency in your life, don't crumble in despair like you're nothing, because you're definitely something! He disciplines those He loves. He invests in you because He intends to use you greatly. Read how Eugene Peterson renders Hebrews 12:5–11:

My dear child, don't shrug off God's discipline, but don't be crushed by it either. It's the child he loves that he disciplines; the child he embraces, he also corrects. God is educating you; that's why you must never drop out. He's treating you as dear children. This trouble you're in isn't punishment; it's training, the normal experience of children. Only irresponsible parents leave children to fend for themselves. Would you prefer an irresponsible God? We respect our own parents for training and not spoiling us, so why not embrace God's training so we can truly live? While we were children, our parents did what seemed best to them. But God is doing what is best for us, training us to live God's holy best. At the time, discipline isn't much fun. It always feels like it's going against the grain. Later, of course, it pays off handsomely, for it's the well-trained who find themselves mature in their relationship with God.

Hebrews 12:5–11 THE MESSAGE

Precious Lord,

I have decided to trust You every step of the way! Have Your way in me. Search me, O God, and know my heart. Test me and know my anxious thoughts. Point out anything in me that offends You and lead me in Your everlasting way. Forgive me for my occasional impatience and shortsightedness. I know that trusting You with every detail of my life is the best thing I can do. Give me a vision for where You're taking me. And help me to be completely faithful in the everyday moments. I will look for You here and I know I will find You. I embrace the process. I know now that when You make me wait it's because You're making me ready. Thank You for Your loving protective care for me. I love You too. Amen.

STUDY QUESTIONS

1. Reread Hebrews 12:5–11 above and answer the following questions:

a. When God points out growth areas in your life, are you more apt to shrug off His words, crumble in a heap underneath them, or take them to heart with humility and confidence? Why?

b. What is God currently saying to you about your character? Your spiritual growth?

c. What does He "sound" like to you (angry, authoritative, distant, kind, up close and personal)?

2. Read Psalm 27:13 and write out this verse as a prayerful declaration for your own life. You *will* see the goodness of the Lord in the land of the living!

3. Read Psalm 27:14 and notice the two directives: Wait on the Lord and take courage. Answer the following questions:

a. On a practical level, what do you personally do to wait on the Lord? Do you turn off the radio in your car? Sit quietly with a cup of tea? Turn off the TV at night? Describe your one process of waiting on God and listening for His voice.

b. What steps do you take to lay hold of fresh courage? When has it been hard to be courageous?

c. According to the verse, what does God promise to do for you?

4. Read 1 Peter 5:6–7 and answer the following questions:

a. How is God asking you to humble yourself before Him in your current season of life?

b. Do you trust that in due time, He will lift you up and establish you? Why or why not?

c. Verse seven calls you to cast your cares on Him, for He cares for you. Write out your cares on a piece of paper. Hold them to your heart, entrust yourself and your cares to God, and then toss your paper in the fireplace (or have a bonfire).

    d. Read verse seven again and write out a prayerful declaration of God's love and care for you.

5. Read and memorize Psalm 62:5, a prayer of faith to the Lord.

6. Read Isaiah 64:4 and consider this: Why is it such a big deal to God when we love and trust Him enough to wait for Him to act? Write down your thoughts.

7. What story from Scripture most stands out to you when it comes to waiting or not waiting on God?

    a. My challenge to you: Write up and share a devotional with one person or with many using the Bible story you listed here; draw truths and insights from the story and from your personal life and talk about the importance of waiting on God.

⸺ DISCUSSION STARTERS ⸺

1. How would you describe your current season of life?

2. What kinds of stories and movies most inspire you and why? Do you notice a theme in those movies that may connect you to God's purpose for you? Explain.

3. What does obedience to God look like for you in this place?

4. If you could step outside your circumstances and look at who you used to be and who God is making you to be, does the person you're becoming encourage you? How so?

5. Share about a time when God put a desire in your heart and then made you wait for its fulfillment.

Face
Your Fears

The Lord says, "I will rescue those who love me. I will protect those who trust in my name. When they call on me, I will answer; I will be with them in trouble. I will rescue and honor them."

Psalm 91:14–15 NLT

I think we had better get free! We must face up to the issues and attitudes and doubts which constitute our fears, that keep us from being happy and victorious Christians. . . . We seem to quake about many things.[1]

—A. W. Tozer

I held on to the podium with a white-knuckled grip and looked out at an audience of two thousand or so. "I'm about to share a very personal story with you. One I never intended to share beyond my mentor and a few close friends. But while preparing for this conference, the Lord strongly nudged me to tell you this part of my story."

I took my hands off the podium and, after a deep breath, released an inward prayer for wisdom and protection.

"Can I ask you to handle what I share with humility and integrity? These are precious pearls to me and I'm still sorting through what God is teaching me here." Then under my breath I mumbled, "I sure hope there are no swine in the audience." Women laughed and I proceeded to unveil a hidden fear that held me captive for many years. One I thought was unique only to me.

As a young girl I'd often go to the grocery store with my mom. I offered her an extra set of hands to push the second cart required to feed our family of nine. On one particular day, my mom and I loaded all of the groceries on the conveyor belt and I worked fast to bag them. Suddenly all of our movement came to a screeching halt. The cashier put her hand up and said, "Um, Mrs. Erickson, we cannot take your check today. Your last one bounced. So sorry."

There we stood with our arms at our sides, broken and embarrassed. We looked at groceries that didn't belong to us and at people who only knew us from a distance. Perfectly and publicly disgraced, we walked out with empty hands and humiliated hearts. Once in the car, my mom put her head on the steering wheel and cried her eyes out.

I sat frozen in the passenger seat, holding my breath and staring at my mom. She gripped the wheel like a life preserver, tears spilling out of her eyes enough to drown her. My heart sank into my stomach like a balled-up fist. Hurt and embarrassed, I ached for her. My parents were good people going through a bad time. But the idea that a private struggle could cause such public humiliation made me privately afraid of being publicly humiliated. From that day on I lived in fear of public disgrace. Over time I developed a knack for striving and for self-preservation.

Jump ahead a bunch of years. A similar experience happened to me. Our medical debt threatened to drown us with more bills than income. I sat with my three little boys in a packed waiting room at the doctor's office. The receptionist yelled out over the busy waiting room, "Mrs. Larson?"

I stood up. "Yes. That's me." She cleared her throat and said loud enough for everyone to hear, "Well, um, we can't see you today. You need to pay more than five dollars on your account every month if you want to see a doctor." Everyone stared at me, waiting for my next move.

Naked and exposed, I gathered my three little ones and headed out to the car. I buckled them up, got in my seat, and put my head on the steering wheel and cried my eyes out.

We had approximately twenty-five-thousand dollars of medical debt. Everyone told us that as long as you paid something, you'd be okay. We paid all of our medical debtors between five and fifteen dollars a month. We barely had enough to spare for food.

Jump ahead a few more years. After listening to my first speaking event on tape, I felt instant nausea. *What had I done? Who do I think I am attempting such a thing?* After listening to the tape, I realized I misspoke on a certain detail of our story. Like a stampede of bulls, the enemy raged in my ear: "You will most certainly dishonor God! You are going to mess this up. I will expose you for the broken mess you are!"

Over the years, several more experiences confirmed my fear of making a mistake and dishonoring God or of falling short and publicly humiliating myself. My humanity combined with painful memories only strengthened the lie within that held me captive.

I worked hard to be a reliable messenger of Christ, meticulous when it came to confirming certain details of a story—partially for integrity's sake, but mostly due to utter fear of getting it wrong.

Even with that paralyzing fear, I walked closely with the Lord. Year after year, layer by layer God revealed my deep need for Him. I enjoyed powerful times of intimacy with God. I lived an abiding life, but unfortunately, for a very long time, I missed out on the abundant life. Some of the best parts of kingdom life eluded me because of my fears.

I lived only partially free even though God moved mightily in our ministry, changing lives at our retreats and conferences and through the messages in my books. On one hand I felt eternally grateful and humbled that God would use me at all, but on the other hand, I felt desperately afraid of success or advancement.

Someone once said, "People will cheer you on as you attempt to climb a mountain, but they're more than happy to shoot you down once you reach the top." Did I really want to step out in faith with all of my baggage? What if I dishonor God? What if I suffer public humiliation?

When I finally admitted my unreasonable fear to a friend, she looked at me like I was an alien. "What are you talking about?" she spouted. "You live cleaner than anyone I know! What's to expose? Why are you listening to the enemy's threats?"

Sometimes a weird look from a friend is a gift straight from heaven. God used her to make me aware of a boulder buried deep in the soil of my heart. A boulder that squished the life out of the seeds planted there. A boulder He intended to dig up.

One morning while getting ready to fly out for a speaking engagement, the Lord surprised me and almost knocked me over with His words. That particular morning I felt happy, ready for the weekend, and my unreasonable fear hadn't reared its head in a while.

Out of nowhere, He spoke these words to me: *I expose the wicked. I protect, defend, and vindicate the righteous. Not because they're perfect but because they're Mine. And you are Mine.*

My eyes instantly filled with tears, blurring my freshly applied mascara. Shocked and surprised, I sucked in a sob and said out loud, "Um, What?"

He whispered those words again. *I expose the wicked. I protect, defend, and vindicate the righteous. Not because they're perfect but because they're Mine. And you are Mine.*

God's words went past my surface happiness and into the depths of my soul. In one surprising moment, the Lord set me free. I knew this truth in my head, but that morning His words made their way into my heart.

As a young girl I watched my teenage sister sit on the bathroom counter with her feet in the sink to apply her makeup. For a lot of years I thought all girls sat on the counter to apply their makeup. To this day, every morning I sit on the counter to apply my makeup.

So there I sat that beautiful morning, with my feet in the bathroom sink, putting on my makeup when the Lord delivered me. With my face inches away from the mirror, I tried to apply mascara but just gave up and cried my eyes out. I couldn't stop.

But I had a plane to catch so I reapplied my makeup. Then I cried it off again. Like a healing balm, God's words played over and over again in my mind, and they completely overwhelmed me. His statement of truth pulled the boulder right out of my soil. I felt raw, delivered, new, and somewhat like I'd just had surgery. I couldn't stop crying. My heart burst with gratitude and absolute wonder that a word of truth could set this prisoner free.

In the days that followed, He unveiled a number of great truths to me.

Without a hint of condemnation, the Lord reminded me of a time when I exposed someone in a way I shouldn't have. She wasn't always a "safe" person to me. She seemed to get her way in unconventional ways. When someone asked me about her methods, I could've steered clear of sharing my opinions, but instead, by asking another question, I insinuated her guilt.

The Lord took me out to the woodshed in the days that followed. I'm not sure if you've ever felt the heavy hand of God's discipline before, but I could barely move for the next three days. My whole body ached with regret and remorse. The enemy, of course, did his best to throw condemnation at me, but it was the Lord's loving and strong conviction that undid me. I rose up from that place of discipline with a whole new fear of God.

Jump ahead to the fresh revelation the Lord gave me regarding my fear of exposure. Without a hint of condemnation, the Lord whispered across my heart: *Do you see how closely linked your fears and your sins are? I love you so much I had to deliver you. It is wrong to cover yourself by uncovering another. I am the One who covers you. Remember, too, I will defend you to others as I defended her to you.*

We Serve a Protective God

Consider Noah. Scripture tells us that when God assigned Noah a task, Noah did *exactly* as the Lord commanded. Exactly. How many of us can testify to such obedience? Then one day Noah passed out drunk and naked. Not his shining hour. Noah's son Ham was the first to see his father. And what was his response? He ran and told.

How often do we respond in the same way?

Noah's two other sons understood honor. They covered their father's nakedness by going into his tent backwards and laying a coat on him. They refused to expose their father; instead, they covered him. And God blessed them for their God-honoring response (see Genesis chapters 5–10).

Jesus defends us not because we're perfect, but because we're His. He loves us with great passion and protection.

When I read about how Ham uncovered his father and exposed him, I pictured God rising up in anger to say, *"That man you're talking about is My son! That naked, drunk man is My beloved Noah! When you expose him, you deal with Me!"*

You wonder if that's true? Read the account of Noah and his sons and pay close attention to the ripple effect of how their choices impacted future generations. Ham's generations reaped the consequence of their father's sin. Shem and Japheth's future generations reaped the blessing of their father's honor. Noah wasn't perfect but he belonged to God.

Know this: God loves you deeply and watches over you with great care. For "whoever touches you touches the apple of His eye" (Zechariah 2:8).

Our fears rise up when we step out. But God will surely defend and deliver us. And He'll lead us to paths of healing and truth. He is serious about our freedom and protective of His investment in us. Sorting through our fears and insecurities is essential to the process of maturing into a woman of significant faith.

We give the enemy opportunity to trip us up again and again when we refuse to deal with our fears and insecurities. We miss out on the redemptive life when we shove our fears below the surface and put on a fake smile.

Just as I watched my sister sit with her feet in the bathroom sink and apply her makeup, I did the same because I understood that's what girls do. We learn at a young age to cover up our imperfections. The problem is, there's not enough makeup in the world to make us whole. If we really want to know true beauty, if we really want to live full and free lives, we have to give God access to those places we work so hard to cover up.

Jesus has no desire to expose our nakedness to a mocking world. He hides us in the shadow of His wing (see Psalm 91:1). He *uncovers* a lie so He can *replace it* with the truth. He puts truth where there once was a lie and we gain credibility and clarity where there once was brokenness and confusion. Psalm 51:6 says, "Behold, You desire truth in the inward parts, and in the hidden part You will make me to know wisdom" (NKJV).

We Are a Threat to the Enemy

Here's something else I learned along the way: The enemy's threat to us is closely linked with our threat to him. A couple days after I filled up the bathroom sink with happy tears, the Lord whispered this question across my heart: *What do you pray every morning for the slave, the oppressed, and the human trafficking victim?*

Without having to think about it, I whispered the prayer I pray every morning and every night: *Lord, expose and frustrate the plans of the wicked and establish the plans of the righteous. Put a firewall between the wicked and the weak! Thwart and intercept the enemy's schemes to victimize the voiceless. In Jesus' name, I pray, amen.*

There was that familiar word again. *Expose* the plans of the wicked. Once more, the Lord had my full attention.

Just a note here: The Lord speaks to each of us in different ways because He knows how to communicate in ways unique to us that we will understand. Jesus said, "My sheep listen to my voice" (John 10:27 NLT). In this place of healing and refinement, He had my ear and I recognized His voice.

He whispered back to me, *Do you see how closely linked your threat to the enemy is with his threat to you? He hates your passions because they are My passions beating in your heart. Let My love cast out your fear, and you'll be a force to reckon with. The devil wants you to connect the dots on certain bad memories so you'll draw wrong conclusions when it comes to your fears. Those wrong conclusions will form a noose around your faith and hold you captive. The only dots I want you connecting are those of My promises! Be hemmed in by My promises, not by your fears!*

The more we gain ground in Christlikeness, the more apt we are to walk out our God-given call and, as a result, the more our lives become a threat to the enemy. The devil hates a transformed life.

Our enemy sees potential in us before we ever see it in our-selves. Think about it. Do you know why a thief robs a home? Because there's good stuff in that home. Scripture calls the devil a thief because he steals, kills, and destroys; he's after all of the good stuff in us (see John 10:10). His worst fear is that you and I will realize our capacity for God's kingdom to flow in and through us. If we come to understand our value, identity, and life-purpose in Christ, the enemy's schemes to diminish our influence or dismantle our call will come to nothing.

Read the following passages and consider how superior to the enemy are God's wisdom and power in our lives. He will protect us:

> "No weapon that has been made to be used against you will succeed. You will have an answer for anyone who accuses you. This is the inheritance of the Lord's servants. Their victory comes from me," declares the Lord.
>
> Isaiah 54:17 GW

> Be strong. Take courage. Don't be intimidated. Don't give them a second thought because God, your God, is striding ahead of you. He's right there with you. He won't let you down; he won't leave you.
>
> Deuteronomy 31:6 THE MESSAGE

> My salvation and my honor depend on God; he is my mighty rock, my refuge. *Trust in him* at all times, you people; pour out your hearts to him, for God is our refuge.
>
> Psalm 62:7–8 emphasis mine

We need to trust Jesus. He's right by our side as we face down our fears. The enemy bullies us with the threat of exposure and humiliation, but our reputation, our honor, and our salvation depend on God alone. Though the enemy sees us as a threat, God sees us as an asset. And God is fully acquainted with our ways. He knows our weaknesses and still chooses to engage us in this kingdom work. In fact, His glory shines brightest in our places of greatest need.

We have to face this fact: We are at war, but overwhelming victory is ours because we belong to Jesus. We overcome the power of the enemy by the blood of the Lamb—and His victory won at the cross—and the word of our testimony—our story, walked out in faith because of Christ's victory (see Revelation 12:11).

We'll Be Transformed Along the Way

By now you can probably sense a little grit in my growl. I believe it's time for women to rise up—not with a feminist chip on our shoulders, but with strength, conviction, humility, and bold perseverance, to be the women God intended us to be. Women who are not . . .

- ∼ constantly bullied by our fears
- ∼ consistently and impossibly insecure and self-aware
- ∼ chronically petty and jealous

Nothing is more beautiful than a strong, humble, God-fearing woman who knows who she is and Whose she is.

If we walk closely with God, we must *expect* Him to change us, heal us, and transform us. As we spend time with Jesus and do what He says, our capacity for His influence in our lives supernaturally increases. May we not only grow more assured that our journey with Christ involves personal transformation, but may we also believe in faith that even at this very moment, God's redemptive purposes are at work in us!

I want you to imagine yourself a year from now walking in a new level of conviction, holy confidence, boldness, and passion. Imagine yourself embracing the days with greater clarity and purpose, choosing more carefully where you put your time because you're convinced more than ever that your life matters.

God will do this work in you to the extent that you entrust yourself to Him.

Let this exhortation from Eric Ludy fill you with faith and courage. It's from a powerful book he coauthored with his wife, Leslie, called *Wrestling Prayer:*

> There is absolutely no excuse to stay where you are at right now. If you are weak, He can make you strong. If you are timid, He can make you brave. If you are a pervert, He can make you pure. If you are selfish, He can make you selfless. If you are a shepherd, He can make you a king. If you are mediocre, He can make you a Mighty One of valor.[2]

Does reaching out to your mean neighbor stir up a fear of rejection? Take your fear to the Lord and see if He won't give you a fresh dose of confidence along with a new heart of compassion. Does stepping up to serve as a greeter at church make you nauseous and want to run the other way? Step up anyway. Ask God for fresh eyes to see those whom He appoints you to touch. You'll be surprised how wonderfully God can love through you. Maybe God is stirring in you to start a Bible study in your neighborhood but you've never led a thing in your life. Remember this: He qualifies those He calls. If you'll walk forward in faith, you will find Him there to meet you every step of the way.

Get a vision for what God wants to do in and through you. Trust Him as He leads you out of your comfort zone and into the faith zone. Don't worry when your fears surface. Just look to the One who takes the power away from our fears and puts redeeming power into our faith. He can make you strong. And He will.

Don't let those past moments of humiliation define you. Don't let them derail you. Let God use those painful, vulnerable experiences from your past to shape you into a woman of bold conviction. Jesus redeems us out of the ashes. And He loves to do so. All glory and honor go to Him.

I cry out to God Most High, to God, who vindicates me. He sends from heaven and saves me, rebuking those who hotly pursue me—God sends forth his love and his faithfulness.

Psalm 57:2–3

Precious Lord,

I humbly bow before You and I thank You for loving me like You do. Teach me to contend with the fears that contend with me! Search me and know me, show me those places of access where the enemy gets in to stir up my fears. Let's shut him down once and for all! I trust You, Lord. I entrust my soul, my hopes, and my dreams to You. Heal every part of me and make me whole. Forgive me for clinging more to my fears than I do to Your promises. Make me a mighty woman of faith. Shine Your light on my face and light up my countenance so when others encounter me, they encounter You. In Jesus' name, I pray. Amen.

STUDY QUESTIONS

1. Prayerfully read Psalm 112 and answer the following questions:

   a. What part of this passage stands out to you and why?

   b. Go through the ten verses and either circle or write down the actions that belong to us (be generous, lend freely, etc.).

   c. Now do the same regarding the actions or promises that belong to God.

   d. Which promise most speaks to your heart? Write it out as a prayerful declaration. Bring that prayerful declaration before the Lord time and time again.

2. Notice verse ten. The whole chapter offers hope and encouragement until we reach verse ten. Why do you suppose we need to be reminded that the wicked rise up against the blessed?

3. While we walk this earth, the enemy will excite the jealousies of others, he'll stir up trouble and aim it at us. He'll work overtime to ignite our fears. What are we to do? Read Psalm 91 and answer the following questions:

    a. What part of this passage stands out to you and why?

    b. Once again, circle or write down the actions that belong to us (do not be afraid, open your eyes, etc.).

    c. Now do the same thing regarding the promises of God.

    d. Write out a prayerful declaration of God's promise to cover and protect you.

4. Read Psalm 27 and do the same thing with this passage:

    a. What part stands out to you and why?

    b. Circle or write down the actions that belong to us.

    c. Circle or write down the actions or promises of God.

    d. Write out a prayerful declaration of God's promise to protect you.

5. Read Isaiah 54:17 and consider the following questions:

    a. Why do you suppose God is so protective of you?

    b. Sometimes when people judge us, they're at least partially right about us. Still, God is the one who deals with us and defends us. What then should your response be to the one who judges you?

6. Based on Psalm 62:7, write down who God is to you and what you possess in Him.

7. Read Psalm 62:8 and consider it a follow-up to verse seven, a reminder that since we are protected, saved, and hidden in God, we can trust Him at all times, with all things. Answer the following questions:

   a. What fear or concern do you need to entrust to His care?

   b. Whose opinion of you carries more weight than it should? Ask God to show you why that is so you can put them back in proper perspective and trust in the name of the Lord for everything you are and everything you do.

⌒ DISCUSSION STARTERS ⌒

1. Can you give an example of a time when, in the face of a fear, you trusted God?

2. How did God show Himself faithful on your behalf?

3. What kinds of things help strengthen your faith and encourage your perspective?

4. What kinds of scenarios trigger fear or self-awareness for you?

5. Whose courage inspires you and why?

6. What's something you wish you had the courage to do?

Hear God's Voice

My sheep listen to
my voice; I know them,
and they follow me.

John 10:27

5

Discern
Your Preparation

We ask God to give you complete knowledge of his will and to give you spiritual wisdom and understanding. Then the way you live will always honor and please the Lord, and your lives will produce every kind of good fruit. All the while, you will grow as you learn to know God better and better.

Colossians 1:9–10 NLT

Never be swayed . . . by what you may see or feel. . . . As you stand firm, your power and experience is being developed, strengthened, and deepened. When you remain unswayed, even in view of supposed contradictions to God's Word, you grow stronger on every front.

—L. B. Cowman[1]

Years ago, the runaway bride in me wanted to cut and run and leave my church because of a relational conflict. I despaired

81

over our differences and even more so over my desire to run and hide. When would I finally learn to hold on to my identity amidst a relational clash? And when would my instinctive response no longer be to cut and run? Around that time my pastor shared this encouraging insight with me: "Don't get discouraged when refining times stir up your fears and flaws and show you your need for more of Jesus. God is just reaching into your soul, grabbing hold of that thing, showing it to you, and saying, 'You see this? I'm about to deliver you from this thing!'" I love that picture.

When the enemy presses in hard to condemn us, we have to remember that we have the authority to shut him down. Luke 10:19 offers this great promise to us: "Look, I have given you authority over all the power of the enemy, and you can walk among snakes and scorpions and crush them. Nothing will injure you" (NLT). In order to still be standing after the battle, we need to know how God has equipped us to fight our battles (see Ephesians 6:16).

After a conversation with my son one day about the refining seasons and the battles we face in life, I envisioned a valley of dry bones—bones from marriages, relationships, and dreams abandoned because many people refused to stand up and fight the right fight, or to humbly die to themselves, and to let God have His way in their lives during times of trial and testing. These people came through the valley with their self-life intact and with their abundant-life-promise dead in the valley. A sad thought, indeed.

Every single Christ-follower is divinely called and appointed to fulfill his or her purpose. But do you know that many Christians will arrive in heaven with almost nothing to show for it? No fruit, no faith risks, no sacrificial giving. Why? Because they chose to cut and run when the going got tough. They chose fear over faith, selfishness over love, and hoarding over giving (see 1 Corinthians 3:13–15).

Jesus came to give us life, and not just any life, a spilling-over abundant, more-than-enough life, one that involves healing, refining, preparation, faith, living for Jesus, and dying to ourselves. One that deeply impacts the world.

How we view our refining times, who we see as the enemy, and how we respond when the going gets tough, is critical not only to our spiritual growth but to how we fare in the days to come. Someone once said, "God has a plan for your life. The devil has a plan for your life. You're the one who casts the deciding vote." Your agreement with God's truths or with the enemy's lies will have a significant impact on how your life unfolds. Do you believe God's promises are true . . . *for you?*

You may have a God-given gift or skill that you long to use in a greater capacity than you are now. You may see other women who seem to have less skill than you but who function at a greater level than you and you privately wonder, *God, why aren't You using me like You're using her?* That's a complicated question, one that deserves more than a surface answer. There's no formula to this. God is all-knowing, all-seeing. Though we may have a sense of our gifts and skill level, God knows the deeper places of our hearts, the places where we're weak or vulnerable.

We may assess our skill or gift and think, *Surely I'm ready for the next level, ready for a promotion.* But our ability is only a small part of the equation. The bigger question is, are we ready to *stand* in that next place? Do we have what it takes to win the battles awaiting us? If God gives us the ground, might we lose it the minute we get pushed around by the enemy? God knows our frame. He knows what's in us. When He makes us wait, it's because He's making us ready. It's not enough to "get there." God wants us to stand there, to win there, and when we're ready, to move on from there to our next place of promise.

God has a protective, loving heart for us. Within each season, He measures out a boundary where we can thrive, flourish, and grow. We have giants to face, battles to win, and victories to gain. These are all doable within the boundaries God sets for us. And the moment He knows we're ready, He'll expand our territory in one way or another.

Maybe you've heard this old adage before: *Personality opens the door. Character keeps it open.* Even truer is this: *As we delight in the Lord, He establishes us* (Psalm 37:23). God puts dreams in our hearts and writes a destiny over our lives. And if we trust Him enough to take Him at His word, we will find ourselves on a journey that prepares us to fulfill that kingdom call.

Unfortunately, the path of promise is often fraught with thickets and thorns. Nothing worth having ever comes easy or without opposition. Storms come, lions roar, and our fears rise up. God allows opposition and training because He knows exactly what our character needs so we'll be able to stand strong in our next place of promise.

And so, as we follow His lead, we will at different times find ourselves in a valley of decision. It's in those places where we can embrace God's beautiful work in our lives, or we can cut and run and do our own thing. Which brings me back to the picture of the valley of bones. It takes humility and faith to persevere through times of testing, to let your flesh die so that your dream can live. Better to leave your self-sins dead in the valley than to leave your dreams there. Here's the test, though: We have a free will and our ways will often seem easier than God's ways, and most of the time, we're free to choose the easier road.

Maybe you're in a job that's all wrong for you, but God has you in that place for a reason. He's using you, changing you, building a gritty perseverance in you, and giving you a new sense of His heart for the hard-to-love in your midst. What do you do? You submit and obey until He tells you differently.

Or maybe you're at a small church serving in a visible role and you'd rather be at a large church serving in a more hidden capacity. You feel out there and exposed, possibly misunderstood and misjudged. But God won't release you to move. What do you do? You stay put until He gives the marching orders move.

Maybe you're serving in a ministry or volunteer capacity where you feel unappreciated and unnoticed. The thought of serving in a more visible, fulfilling way seems a treasured option, but all you hear is God's whisper, *Trust me here. I have things to teach you here. Humble yourself and faithfully serve Me in this place.* What are you to do? You trust Him in this place and believe that He knows what's absolutely best for you. Remember, when He makes you wait, it's because He's making you ready.

Hold On to Your Identity

What's painful about these times is that they tend to bring out the worst in us. Why would God want us in a place where our self-life seems to upstage the God-life in us? If you're in this place, do remember, God is near you. He loves and adores you, and He will not abandon you no matter how you may feel about yourself at the moment.

Another painful reality about this training process is the spiritual battle associated with our preparation. It's in these refining times the enemy finds us easy targets for accusation, condemnation, and discouragement. He intends to parade our flaws and foibles in front of us in hopes to convince us that our desperate need disqualifies us from any kind of significant calling. But thanks be to God, He saves us and establishes us through grace. The power of God's love brings provision to those very places of our pressing need. His kingdom is powerfully at work in us where we need Him most. Remember what Scripture says regarding our weaknesses:

> "My grace is sufficient for you, for my power is made perfect in weakness." Therefore I will boast all the more gladly about my weaknesses, so that Christ's power may rest on me. That is why, for Christ's sake, I delight in weaknesses, in insults, in

hardships, in persecutions, in difficulties. For when I am weak, then I am strong.

2 Corinthians 12:9–10

I remember as a little girl, sitting with my dad, watching from the kitchen window as my older brother battled it out in our yard with the neighborhood bully. The bully seemed to have the upper hand, but my brother didn't give up. Anxiously I tugged on my dad's sleeve and said, "Daddy, why don't you go save him? What if he loses? Go help him!"

Keeping his eyes fixed on my brother, he gently yet firmly replied, "If he doesn't face down this bully, he'll always have to deal with him. I won't let him lose, but I have to let him fight."

I'll never forget that moment. Jesus won't let us lose, but He has to let us fight. Jesus is always with us. Overwhelming victory is ours because of Him. He gave us armor so we can stand amidst the enemy's threats and taunts. Your mean boss is not the enemy; your disengaged husband is not the enemy; your divisive neighbor is not the enemy. The devil himself is your enemy, and you have everything you need to put him and his power under your feet.

Remember, you don't have to be mighty in stature to be mighty in battle. You don't have to be beautiful or strong, or even physically fit to change the world, you just have to know that far greater is He that is in you than he that is in the world (see 1 John 4:4). Ephesians 3:20 tells us that He wants to do abundantly above and beyond all that we could ever ask or think, but there's a clincher in this verse . . . it's *according* to His work *within us*. To the extent that He's allowed to work in us, will be the extent that He does great things through us.

Training Time for Reigning Time

If we don't see our trials as "training time for reigning time,"[2] we will look for the quickest way out of the worst parts of our trial and thus find ourselves wandering in the wilderness instead of moving toward God's promise for us.

Oftentimes our current obstacles, setbacks, and trials seem totally unrelated to the call of God on our lives, so they're easy to misinterpret. And yet they're an important part of our maturing process. In fact it's easy to think, *I'd be living out my call if I didn't have to deal with* this *issue*. But the thing is, whatever "this issue" is, it's your training ground—testing and proving you, preparing you for a life of depth and significance. No matter how uncomfortable you may feel at the moment, you must know that God is able to make all grace abound to you in this place, so you, having all that you need, will abound in every circumstance and situation (see 2 Corinthians 9:8).

Is His kingdom real to you in this place? It can be. Like my pastor once said, "You're not free to go until you're free to stay." Call on God until His power invades your reality. Seeking out and finding His kingdom power here will equip you to seek and find it in the next place He has for you.

God so wants to use you. Let Him do a mighty work in you.

Here are some common training grounds God uses to train His people to last long and finish strong:

∽ *Betrayal and Relational Difficulty:* How will you deal with it if a close friend or colleague betrays you? How is your view of God and of your own identity affected when you have family conflict? How will you respond? Will you bless or curse? Will you forgive or hold a grudge? Will you look down or look up? Someone else's betrayal is not your barrier to a full and fruitful life. Another person's negative assessment of you cannot keep you from God's best for you. What the enemy means for evil, God can always use for good. Allow God to use this opportunity to teach you deep and loving forgiveness, humble and gracious mercy, and strong and courageous boundaries when needed. Allow this difficult circumstance to shape you into the Christlike, holy-confident individual He destined you to be.

Training Principle: Entrust your soul to the Most High God.

So humble yourselves under the mighty power of God, and at the right time he will lift you up in honor.

1 Peter 5:6 NLT

∾ *Financial Hardship:* How will you respond to financial hardship? Will you panic and grab for yourself? Will you quit tithing and refuse to notice those who have less than you? Or will you remember once again that your help comes from the Lord and that He supplies your need out of the riches of His storehouse? Most every great Christian I've met has experienced a time of financial uncertainty at some point. In God's grace, He uses such times to help us shift our trust from earthly security to His promise to provide for us. In every season, whether in plenty or in scarcity, we are called to flow through accounts of God's blessing to a world in need.

Training Principle: Trust God for every single need.

And this same God who takes care of me will supply all your needs from his glorious riches, which have been given to us in Christ Jesus.

Philippians 4:19 NLT

∾ *Being Overlooked:* While you're in the training process, you may feel invisible at times. God may use you in a profound or powerful way just when the "right" people are looking the wrong way. Has that ever happened to you? They look right past you as if you didn't exist. They don't see you for the mighty kingdom woman you are.

Sometimes it's not intentional. Give *them* the benefit of the doubt, but tell the enemy, "Devil, I know you intended to hurt me, to make me feel dismissed and less-than. I reject what you're saying to me here. God has a mighty plan for my life and at just the right time, I'll lay hold of it."

My girlfriend Stephanie once said, "What appears to be rejection is most times God's protection. Move forward trusting that God has a better plan for you."

When God uses you but others ignore you, you can respond in one of two ways: You can stomp your foot and spout, "Did You see *me*? I'm legitimate!" or you can humbly declare, "God, I see You. I know You see me. And one day, You'll establish me."

Training Principle: Trust that God sees you and has a great plan for your life.

> I remain confident of this: I will see the goodness of the Lord in the land of the living.
>
> Psalm 27:13

꙳ *Disillusionment With Ministry, an Organization, or Church:* You will most likely walk through a time of frustration or disillusionment with a ministry, an organization, or your local church during your training time. The question becomes, will you maintain dignity and honor while you wrestle with what offends you? Remember the story of Noah's sons from chapter 4? Even if you have some legitimate frustrations and you observe some obvious flaws in another ministry, will you uncover their nakedness by gossiping about it? Or will you humbly bow in intercession, and pray for mercy and God's influence where things are wrong, just as you'd want someone to do for you? William MacDonald wrote these cautionary, wise words:

In essentials, unity. In doubtful questions, liberty. In all things, charity. There is enough of the flesh in every one of us to wreck any local church or any other work of God. Therefore, we must submerge our own petty, personal whims and attitudes, and work together in peace for the glory of God and for common blessing.[3]

A quick side note here: Sometimes you're called to speak up and address a wrong. Don't go into that battle without much humble prayer and wise God-fearing counsel. But biblical confrontation is different from spewing and spouting your assessments to anyone who will listen. Also, don't assume everyone is guilty by association. Most likely there are intercessors on the inside that are praying fervently for a turnaround. Pray that those who fear God will be established in that place. How you handle ministry disillusionment says a lot about your readiness for promotion.

Training Principle: No matter how others behave, you walk in the fear of the Lord.

> Whoever goes about slandering reveals secrets, but he who is trustworthy in spirit keeps a thing covered.
>
> Proverbs 11:13 ESV

∽ *Past Baggage:* Sometimes when God is about to do a new thing, the devil will bring up an old thing because he wants us looking back when we should be looking up. There's got to be a point when we stop in our tracks and declare, "I command these inferior thoughts of past sins to come under the authority of Jesus Christ. I will not allow my past to speak to me except to teach me!" Are you able to do what Scripture says and forget what lies behind and look forward to what lies ahead (see Philippians 3:13)? You cannot lay hold of the fresh promise of God if your hands are wrapped around an old lie.

Training Principle: Forget what lies behind and look forward to what lies ahead. God is doing a new thing!

Therefore, there is now no condemnation for those who are in Christ Jesus.

Romans 8:1

~ *Someone Else's Blessing:* As you wait for the Lord to establish His purposes in you, can you consider the in-between time an opportunity to cultivate intimacy with and trust in your heavenly Father? How we respond to someone else's blessings says a lot about where our affections lie. I failed this test miserably but somehow still came through it more acquainted with Jesus. He graced me every step of the way.

We'd just moved back to our home state after living out of state for a year. Kevin and I weren't in a position to purchase a home because of our medical debt. We lived with Kevin's parents for six weeks. Then a friend told us about a home for rent. Though grateful for a place to live, over time I longed for a place to call our own.

The walls of our rented house were all a pale yellow color (which over time reminded me of pee), and the carpet was a dull beige. Though God blessed us with a place to live and I had every reason to give thanks, it seemed my whole life lacked color. Discontentment crept its way into my soul. Eventually the doctor diagnosed me with mild depression (which lasted about a year). We'd walked through years of crisis, health, and financial battles leaving me a rootless, weary traveler, while so many of my friends seemed established in their lives.

During that time I met a new friend who had three boys like I did, but she also had a beautiful little girl to boot (I so wanted a little girl, but due to endometriosis, I needed a full hysterectomy at age twenty-nine). We lived on one side of the highway and she on the other, where all the rolling hills and big, beautiful homes seemed to be. Her husband worked mostly from home and had lots of time for the family. My husband worked two, sometimes three jobs, and we still couldn't seem to make ends meet.

In every way, she lived the life I wanted. I loved this family. They love Jesus and were nothing but generous and kind. My misery was my problem.

One night Kevin and I packed up our kids and headed across the highway to their beautiful home. Several families gathered there that night for food, winter sledding, and games. We got out of the car and I padded up to the house. I paused in the front yard and looked up at this stately Victorian two-story house. I noticed the frilly curtains that framed the windows from the inside and the candles that made them glow. An instant lump filled my throat. Just then my middle son, Luke, joyfully shouted, "Hey, Mom, watch out!" I turned around and an ice ball hit me right in the temple. Luke had playfully thrown a snowball at me, not realizing how hard it would hit me.

Instantly I dropped to my knees on the snow. I put my face in my hands and filled them with tears.

Lukey rushed up to me, put his snow-covered mittens around my neck, and said, "Oh, Momma, I'm so sorry! I didn't mean to hit you so hard."

I wrapped him up in a hug and forced back my tears. I said, "It's not you, honey, it's me. Let's go in and have some fun." But I just wanted to go back across the highway to my rented home. I didn't feel much like taking in the sights and cinnamon scents of my friend's amazing life. I stood up, brushed the snow off of my pants, and stepped up to the front door. I greeted my new friend with a weak smile, a runny nose, red eyes, and a newly formed lump on the side of my head.

I had a perfectly miserable time. By the time we got back home that night, I didn't have words to express the grief and sadness I felt. I think the load of all the difficult years combined are what weighed so heavy on my heart that night. The life I longed for and the life I'd lived seemed a great distance apart. Kevin and I sat on the couch side by side once we got the children tucked in for the night. He reached over and grabbed my hand. I put my head on his shoulder and, with tears streaming down my cheeks, we prayed a passage from Habakkuk:

> Though the fig tree does not bud and there are no grapes on the vines, though the olive crop fails and the fields produce no food, though there are no sheep in the pen and no cattle in the stalls, yet I will rejoice in the Lord, I will be joyful in God my Savior.
>
> 3:17–18

That prayer of surrender ushered healing to my soul. Peace and grace came in like a flood and I knew God had me in this place for a purpose. *Oh, Lord,* I prayed, *have Your way in me.*

Our Hope Is in the Lord

We need these painful times of refining so we will know in the depths of our being (where most lies go to hide), that our hope is in the Living God who daily establishes His purposes for us. Our hope is not in people, financial provision, acceptance or popularity, a local church or particular ministry, or even a beautifully decorated cinnamon-scented home. Our hope is in the living, loving God who has our hand, our heart, and our dreams very close to His heart.

If you're in a season of refining, *lean in.* Trust the loving hand of your precious Savior and know that He will lead you to the other side. Refuse a sense of entitlement and don't demand to be understood. Instead, humble yourself and seek to understand what the Lord is doing around you. He will faithfully lead you and He'll strengthen you as you go. On the other side of this refining time is a fresh perspective and new mercies. Humble yourself under the mighty hand of God; in due time you will be lifted up and honored before a watching world.

> Everyone's going through a refining fire sooner or later, but you'll be well-preserved, protected from the eternal flames. Be preservatives yourselves. Preserve the peace.

Mark 9:49–50 THE MESSAGE

Precious Lord,

You are always good. Thank You for loving me like You do. Help me to see You in my current life circumstance. Open up my eyes to see the wonder of Your love, the riches of Your grace, and the beauty of Your plan for me. I open up my hands to You and say with all my heart, You get to decide, Lord. You get to decide the how, the when, and the what for the deepest desires of my heart. Pour Your Spirit out on me. Give me grit and grace to lean in and learn everything I can in this place. I belong to You, Lord. We shall never be apart, and for this, I'm forever grateful. Amen.

STUDY QUESTIONS

1. Read James 1:2–4 and make its application to your own life:

   a. What "many trials" are you facing right now?

   b. In what ways is your faith being tested (what are you tempted to believe or disbelieve because of your current trial)?

   c. How is your need for perseverance impacting your character?

   d. As best as you can discern, why do you suppose this trial is "necessary" in your life?

2. Read James 1:12 and answer the following questions:

   a. Why do you suppose God rewards in heaven those who've persevered on earth?

   b. Not everyone perseveres or "stands the test." Make your best guess here: Can you give a few examples of the kinds of thoughts that open the door for those who decide to give up and quit?

   c. How then should one reinforce their thought life and guard their hearts against discouragement?

3. Read James 1:5–8 and write out a prayer, asking God for wisdom for your current situation. Go boldly before the throne of grace and ask for lavish amounts of grace, peace, provision, and power to walk valiantly through your circumstances.

   a. Remember from chapter 2 that to doubt is to see two ways instead of one? Look again at this passage from James 1:5–8 and determine to believe that God will bring the revelation that you need. Write out a prayer declaring God's faithfulness and your trust in Him.

4. Read 1 Peter 5:8–9 and answer the following questions:

   a. What does it mean to be alert and of sober mind? Do you need to make any life adjustments so you can be alert and sober, and not caught off guard?

   b. Verse 9 offers two important reminders: With the authority of Christ in you, you can resist the devil and make him stand down. And you are not alone. Which of those points are you most apt to forget?

   c. What will you do to keep perspective?

5. Read 1 Peter 5:10–11 and write out a prayer of thanksgiving—by faith—that you serve a God of breakthroughs and restoration.

6. Read James 4:7 and answer the following questions:

   a. How is God asking you to submit to Him (and what steps are you taking to obey Him)?

   b. How is the enemy coming against you right now (and what are you doing to stand against him, to resist him)?

   c. Why do you suppose we need to submit to God first, and then resist the enemy?

   d. When you humbly submit to God and you resist the enemy, what can you *expect* to happen? Do you possess that expectancy? Do you understand what kind of authority you possess? (If not, ask God to give you greater understanding of your authority in Him.)

7. Read Ephesians 6:10–16 and answer the following questions:

   a. What do you think it means to *be strong in the Lord and in His mighty power*? Since we're called to be strong, what must we do to be strong?

   b. Part of the answer to the question above is found in verse 11. Why do we need the armor of God for this fight? (Hint: Verse 12 gives us the answer.)

   c. Write down the different pieces of armor and a practical example of why you need them and how you'd use them.

⟨⟩ DISCUSSION STARTERS ⟨⟩

1. Of the training grounds identified in this chapter, is there one that most speaks to you? Why?

2. What do you sense God is trying to teach you in your current circumstances?

3. Looking back over your life, what trial most trained you to walk in the place God has you now?

4. Looking back over the past year, have you noticed a change in your spiritual life? (e.g., Do you have firmer faith, greater perspective, more love, a more active prayer life?) What has been the biggest catalyst to your spiritual growth?

5. Where do you want to be, and who do you want to be a year from now?

6

Silence
Your Enemy

I focus on this one thing: Forgetting the past and looking forward to what lies ahead, I press on to reach the end of the race and receive the heavenly prize for which God, through Christ Jesus, is calling us.

Philippians 3:13–14 NLT

If you are still wrapped in grave clothes and great fears lie upon you, it is time for you to dare to rise and in sweet faith in the risen Jesus Christ declare: "I will not take this any longer. I am a child of God—why should I go mourning all the day?"[1]

—A. W. Tozer

Whenever we venture out to take new land or to fulfill part of God's purpose for us, opposition comes. The enemy predictably stirs up fears, brings up old failures, and throws a wet blanket of condemnation to extinguish our fiery passion. Without fail, the enemy meets our forward movement with opposition tailored specifically to us to undo us. He aims to take our eyes off of Christ and to knock our feet out from under us. Like Joyce Meyer often says, "New level, new devil."

One night as I tucked my oldest son into bed, he asked, "If the devil doesn't know the future, how does he know to step up his attack right before God is about to do something great?" For a ten-year-old, his insight surprised me.

I sat back and thought about it for a moment, whispered a prayer for wisdom, and said the only thing that came to mind. "Do you remember the story of when Elisha prayed for his servant's eyes to open so he could see God's presence in their midst? God opened the servant's eyes to show him the hills covered with horses and chariots of fire. I think, when the enemy sees the cavalry mounting on our behalf, he steps up his threats and taunts because he knows that *we* can't see the forces that stand behind us. He knows that we're probably not aware of how close we are to victory."

It's taken me years to learn this lesson, but I finally understand (at least most of the time) that whenever the enemy throws a lie my way, I can pretty much know that the opposite is true. Have you ever battled with the following lies? I hope the truths that follow encourage you:

- *You're worthless!* Actually, I'm worth everything to the One who can squish you like a bug.
- *If you keep moving forward, I'll attack you on every side!* Actually, God has given me all authority over *you*, so you'll do what I tell you to, in Jesus' name.
- *Your worst fears are about to come true!* The Bible tells me to fear nothing except the Lord Almighty. If I fear Him, I need fear nothing else.
- *Your breakthrough will never come.* Well, the fact that you're taking the time to bother with me makes me think

the opposite is true. In fact, any day now, I expect to see God move in my midst.

∾ *No one likes you!* Jesus loves me, and I resemble Him more today than I did yesterday. Even when your lies *feel* true, God's Word *is* true, and I choose to believe Him over you.

One of my favorite pastimes is cycling on the bike trails as fast as I can, especially on a hot and humid day. With an ear bud in one ear and my other ear open to the sounds of birds singing (and traffic), I pound out the trails listening to Steven Curtis Chapman's "Live Out Loud," Mandisa's "Dance, Dance, Dance," and a long list of other wonderful upbeat songs.

I love how the trees whip by me in a blur, my lungs scream for air, and my forehead drips with sweat. One of the best things about riding the trails is the breathtaking scent of freshly bloomed flowers, plants, and trees. I'm continually amazed at how God managed to come up with individual scents that blend so beautifully together. I suppose that after spending so much time sick in bed, my times on the trails are a flag-in-the-ground declaration that God has restored me.

One morning before heading to work, I decided to hop on my bike for some me time. The blue sky and bright sun shouted my invitation to hit the trails. I buckled my helmet, put on my riding gloves, reset my odometer, and pedaled out of the driveway. I lifted my head, took in a deep cleansing breath, and almost gagged. The stench of filth and garbage overwhelmed me. I looked down the block and spied a garbage truck about twenty houses away. That its smell still lingered in front of my house surprised me.

I tried to hold my breath as I pedaled toward the bike paths. Yet every time the truck opened its mouth, a new wave of stench filled the hot, humid air. It didn't matter that the sky was a beautiful blue, it didn't matter that my bike fit me perfectly or that I had some free time to enjoy a ride, the smell of garbage contaminated the beauty of that God-given moment. I couldn't stand it anymore so I gripped my handlebars, put my head down, and sprinted down the block until I passed the smelly beast. I finally had a beautiful, soul-nourishing ride ahead of me.

Scripture describes the enemy as a liar, an accuser, and the source of confusion. Every time he opens his mouth, stench fills the air. If we allow him to stay in front of us speaking his filth and defeat, it won't matter if our call fits us perfectly or if God gives us time and space to fulfill it. The putrid smell of the enemy's presence will poison the beauty of the day. Garbage is yesterday's news. New mercies are ours today. It's time to tell that foul-mouthed enemy to get behind us so we can face our future with hope and expectancy.

No Condemnation for Us Who Are in Christ Jesus

Every day on the way to the radio station, I use the drive time to pray for the show. I pray for the listeners (that they'll be healed, restored, strengthened, and mobilized). I pray for my readers (that you'll be healed, restored, strengthened, and mobilized). I pray for my walk of faith, that I will rightly divide the Word of truth, that I will walk blamelessly before the Lord and serve Him with a pure heart, and that I will last long and finish strong. I don't take calls during that time because it's a time set aside to intercede for those God has given me to serve. My morning devotional time is for studying God's Word, praying for social issues around the world, aligning my thoughts with God, interceding for family and friends, and so on.

One day during my drive to the station, I suddenly felt bogged down by a lack of peace and joy. My prayers seemed sluggish and heavy, like I couldn't fling them up to heaven, let alone get them off the ground. God felt far away. *Lord, what's this about?* I wondered. I turned on the radio and began to sing. Within a few minutes, Romans 8:1 passed through my mind:

> Therefore, there is now no condemnation for those who are in Christ Jesus.

I stayed quiet a little longer, and the Lord whispered this assurance to me: *That's right, My child, there's now no condemnation, no root, no weed, no seed in you. I have set you free from the law of sin and death. There's no spot of sin on you. No past mistake will ever mar your beauty again. When I see you, I see a cleansed and beautiful creation. There's no stain on you. Do not allow the enemy to throw his dirt at you. Do not view yourself covered with smudges of past sins. They're gone. Wiped clean. When I say no condemnation, I mean no condemnation.*

I'm not sure why I missed it before, but I never really considered the idea that no condemnation actually means *no* condemnation. None.

For years I've walked through life picturing my righteous robe slightly smudged here and a little smeared there with dirt from my past sins and offenses, and the nagging sense that—truth be told—I am only mostly clean. I know now I'm not the only one bogged down by this lie. Whenever we talk of condemnation or of regrets on the show, the phone lines light up. I'd say it's time to lay hold of a life free of condemnation.

Life in the Spirit

Jesus canceled the written code against us, He made a public spectacle of the powers that oppose us, and He dismantled the enemy's plan to destroy us. In fact, Jesus redefined the meaning of the cross. He went to the place of utter public humiliation and scorn, to the place where guilty men die, and He won our victory *there*. If you look a few verses down from Romans 8:1, you'll find this profound nugget of truth:

> Those who live according to the flesh have their minds set on what the flesh desires; but those who live in accordance with the Spirit have their minds set on what the Spirit desires. The mind governed by the flesh is death, but the mind governed by the Spirit is life and peace.

8:5–6

Now, initially when we think of having our minds set on what the flesh desires, we think of drinking too much, eating too much, watching too much TV, or maybe even worse things than these. And that's a correct application to this verse, but it goes beyond choices of excess. We live according to the flesh when our thoughts replay deeds done in the flesh. Our flesh likes to feed on flesh, gross as that may sound. Our flesh is bent toward the deeds of the flesh. So when we who are in Christ Jesus replay our past sins over and over again, we are actually functioning "in the flesh."

According to the verse above, the mind governed by the flesh leads to death, in this case, death to our dreams, our peace, our joy, our perspective. Living under condemnation even impairs our prayers. If we start out praying from a wrong position of unbelief regarding the basic truth of our identity and position in Christ, our prayers will lack power and influence.

Look again at the Romans 8:5–6 passage above and consider this: Flesh gives birth to more of the flesh; spirit gives birth to more of God's Spirit. Anything born of the flesh is destined for death; anything born of the Spirit has eternal wings and flies from this life to the next. This applies to every area of the believer's life: our thoughts, our service, our ambitions, and our motives. Even the way we love. If our actions are born out of our fleshly striving, self-preservation, and unbelief, we'll cause more harm than good.

But if what we do springs from that abiding place of intimacy with God, life and peace will abound, in this life and the next.

Read William MacDonald's powerful insight on the law of sin and death and the law of Spirit of life in Christ Jesus:

> It's like the law of gravity. When you throw a ball into the air, it comes back down because it is heavier than the air it displaces. A living bird is also heavier than the air it displaces, but when you toss it up in the air, it flies away. *The law of life in the bird overcomes the law of gravity.* So the Holy Spirit supplies the risen life of the Lord Jesus, making the believer free from the law of sin and death.[2]

The life of Christ within us puts us *above* our circumstances, above our pasts, even above our low perception of ourselves. Whether it feels true or not, Christ's sacrifice—His overwhelming victory on the cross—gave us a brand-new identity, one that's renewed day by day.

We must walk in the newness of our identity if we hope to live life abundantly. It's the best witness to a world weighed down by the gravity of life. And when we come before the living God with a right understanding of who we are and what we possess in Him, we start to see answers to our prayers, victory in our battles, and a greater ability to discern and shut down the enemy's lies. Peace, life, and forward movement are all a part of the life God promised us, as pastor Jim Cymbala writes:

> Personal peace is a quality of the Promised Land that God is bringing us into. It is part of the greater blessing he intends for our lives. He cannot stand the thought of us succumbing to accusations, animosities, anxieties, and a bad mental atmosphere. He is calling us to something higher—a life infused with the supernatural peace of God. We must arise and receive this wonderful provision from his hand.[3]

May we all memorize the following verse and pull it out like a sword whenever the enemy tries to condemn us: "I have been

crucified with Christ and *I no longer live, but Christ lives in me.*
The life I now live in the body, I live by faith in the Son of God, who
loved me and gave himself for me" (Galatians 2:20, emphasis mine).

Conviction, Not Condemnation

Dear friends, if our hearts do not condemn us, we have confidence before God and receive from him anything we ask, because
we keep his commands and do what pleases him. And this is his
command: to believe in the name of his Son, Jesus Christ, and
to love one another as he commanded us.

1 John 3:21–23

Years ago, at a certain time in my life, my prayers seemed to
bounce off the ceiling and my heart was only half in it. I didn't
want to ask God about my lackluster prayers because I already
knew my problem: I had a grudge against my husband. I loved
Kevin and didn't want to be with anybody else but him, but his
workaholism wearied me so and I couldn't see any light at the
end of the tunnel.

Eventually my love for Jesus upstaged my desire to nurse a
sore heart. I got down on my knees and asked forgiveness for
keeping an account against my husband when Christ kept no
account on me. I surrendered my feisty self to the Lord once
again. I entrusted my marriage and Kevin to Him as well. I
prayed a prayer of blessing on my honey and on our marriage.
And the peace returned.

If we allow attitudes of cynicism, judgment, or unforgiveness to seep into our lives, we pollute our peace and joy. As
Christ-followers, we're not allowed the option of unforgiveness
or the luxury of a bad attitude. Nothing diminishes our spiritual
growth like a divided heart.

Without realizing it, we sometimes try to live with one foot
in the Spirit and one in the law. Our offender's list should be

nailed to the cross, but we'd rather keep it in our hands to recount again and again. As Christians, we must accept that the things done to us, along with the things we've done, are together on the cross.

It goes without saying that a central part of a thriving, intimate walk with God involves immediately responding in faith to the guidance of the Holy Spirit within us, obeying when He so nudges us, and repenting of sin as soon as we're aware of it. If we walk in disobedience to God and we disregard His command to love our fellowman, no degree of standing against the accusations of the devil will bring us peace. The Holy Spirit invites us to obey in order to strengthen our faith and grow us in love, and He convicts us of sin to draw us back into a right relationship with Christ again.

Let's look at the first part of 1 John 3:21 again: *"If our hearts do not condemn us, we have confidence before God."* If we feel unsettled in our spirits, without peace, and lack confidence before God, we can consider one of two reasons:

- ∿ We've sinned or disobeyed and we need to get right with God. "If we confess our sins, he is faithful and just and will forgive us our sins and purify us from all unrighteousness" (1 John 1:9).
- ∿ We're listening to the lies of the enemy, who tries continuously to move us out from under grace and put us back under the law (which he has no legal right to do). *"Submit yourselves, then, to God. Resist the devil, and he will flee from you"* (James 4:7). *"We demolish arguments and every pretension that sets itself up against the knowledge of God, and we take captive every thought to make it obedient to Christ"* (2 Corinthians 10:5).

Scripture says we can approach the throne of grace with boldness and confidence, assured of the Lord's glad welcome. Jesus gives us right standing with God. But if our conscience bothers us, either because we've ignored our sin or we've listened to lies, we'll have no confidence when we come before God.

Did you know that when we go to prayer, we actually approach the throne of grace, our Intercessor Christ Jesus, and a host of promises that are yes and amen to us (see 2 Corinthians 1:20)? If the devil can keep us earthbound and self-focused, we'll miss out on appropriating the riches of heaven available to us at this very moment, riches that renew us and enable us to thrive in a fallen world.

Warren Wiersbe shares this wonderful insight on 1 John 3:19–20: "No Christian should treat sin lightly, but no Christian should be harder on himself than God is. There is a morbid kind of self-examination and self condemnation that is not spiritual."[4]

Our Part, God's Part

Just how do we put our past regrets, sins, and shame behind us? How do we silence the enemy's harassment and live free of condemnation? We believe to the depths of our being that Jesus paid our whole debt. And then, we reinforce our freedom and right standing by engaging our faith. It doesn't matter if people have outdated opinions of us. Jesus has an updated one, and His mercies are new every morning. Our right standing in Christ exempts us from condemnation, and our shield of faith raised high blocks every foul insult the enemy sends our way.[5]

Here's another powerful piece of advice right out of Hebrews 12:1–3:

> Therefore, since we are surrounded by such a great cloud of witnesses, let us throw off everything that hinders and the sin that so easily entangles. And let us run with perseverance the race marked out for us, fixing our eyes on Jesus, the pioneer and perfecter of faith. For the joy set before him he endured

the cross, scorning its shame, and sat down at the right hand of the throne of God. Consider him who endured such opposition from sinners, so that you will not grow weary and lose heart.

Do you want to give the enemy less fodder with which to attack you? Do you want to be fierce when it comes to walking in abundant-life freedom and identity? Throw off everything that hinders you in your pursuit of Christ. Let your conscience be clear before the Lord. Toss aside those things that are not necessarily sin in themselves but slow you down and turn your attentions elsewhere. And get rid of the obvious sin that predictably trips you up again and again.

Understand, though, that conquering habitual sin can be an uphill climb. We so often do the very things we hate, and then we hate ourselves for it. We stumble and fall, and the enemy kicks us with condemnation when we're down.

It's not an easy fight, but remember this: Grace surrounds us.

Jesus is a friend of sinners. When we've done a face-plant in the dirt because of our own selfishness or personal weakness, He picks us up off the gravel, dusts us off, and wraps His arms around us. He strengthens and sanctifies us as we go. He loves us more than He hates our sin. He'll not forsake us on this journey.

Since His love and abundant-life promise is true, do not relent when it comes to the things in your life that trip you up again and again. Pray. Repent of your sin. Renounce your attachment to it. Renew your resolve to walk freely with Christ. And then do the same tomorrow if you have to. Walk on until you walk free. You can't lose with Jesus on your side.

Jesus used the cross, a place of utter shame and public humiliation, to display His love and power for mankind. He turned the tables on the enemy. Because of Him we can now redefine our circumstance. We can stand against the enemy's threats, taunts, and accusations and actually bring dignity, honor, and power to our places of struggle. We can walk humbly and boldly because the power of the Living God is mightily at work within us.

Jesus cheers for us every day. He intercedes on our behalf. He sees us without a hint of stain or sin. Jesus is profoundly dear to the Father's heart because He endured hell to keep you and me from it. The cross didn't win. Jesus won. And we are the benefactors. Amazing grace.

We really have no comprehension of just how secure we are in Christ. Oh, may we grasp how strong our position is in Him! These words from an old hymn by W. N. Tomkins capture it beautifully:

> Reach my blest Savior first,
> Take Him from God's esteem;
> Prove Jesus bears one spot of sin,
> Then tell me I'm unclean.[6]

In modern-day language, this verse declares: *You want to accuse me? Well, you have to go through my Savior first. I dare you to try and take Him away from His father's loving affections. You'll never succeed. I dare you to find one spot or stain on my pure and spotless Lamb of God. You can't, can you? Since you can't find a spot on Him, you'll not find a spot on me!*

May we walk in a whole new assurance of the finished work of Christ. When He said, "It is finished!" He meant it. Praise God.

Keep walking. Keep trusting. Keep declaring the promises of God over your life. Daily affirm your secure identity in Christ based on His finished work on the cross, period. Daily, humbly submit yourself, your cares, and your attitudes to the living God. And when the enemy comes in like a flood, engage your faith, knowing full well that you have all authority—all of heaven on your side—and make that wretched liar flee. To the extent that we lay hold of our secure position in Christ, will we be able to stand strong against the enemy's lies. Jesus overcame. Now we can overcome.

You, dear children, are from God and have overcome them, because the one who is in you is greater than the one who is in the world.

1 John 4:4

Precious Lord,

Thank You for the cross. Thank You for leaving the comforts of heaven, for enduring unimaginable suffering, for defeating sin and death, just so You could come and rescue me. Help me to put my past behind me because You've already put it behind You. My salvation and honor are in Your hands. If I can trust You with my eternity, I can trust You with my identity. Oh, how I love You, Lord. I embrace by faith, the freedom and abundant life You secured for me. Amen.

STUDY QUESTIONS

1. Read Colossians 3:1 and answer the following question:

   a. What aspects of your life feel unredeemed, like they've not yet been "raised with Christ"?

2. What do you think are the "realities of heaven," and how do you suppose they might impact your life down here?

   a. What areas in your life make it difficult to set your sights on things above? What do you sense God saying to you regarding your perspective in these areas?

   b. Consider the significance for you that Christ sits in a place of honor in heaven. Why is that important with regard to your identity, your calling, and your standing before God here on earth?

3. Read Colossians 3:2–3 and answer the following questions:

   a. What do you think it means to live a life hidden in God?

b. What aspects of your life pull you out of that hidden place?

4. I'd like you to revisit James 4:7 again.

a. Spend a moment humbling yourself under the mighty hand of God. Ask Him to search your heart and point out any door you've opened to the enemy.

b. Based on what God shows you during your time of prayer, ask the Lord's forgiveness. Then accept His forgiveness, and by faith, shut the doors He speaks to you about (critical attitude, negative thinking, disobedience, unforgiveness, etc.).

c. Now it's time to stand up in your authority, raise your shield, and resist the enemy's lies. Under Christ's authority, the enemy *has* to flee. Write out a prayerful declaration; stand against the enemy's threats and declare God's faithfulness to you.

5. Read Romans 8:1 and rewrite this verse to make it personal by inserting your name.

6. Read Romans 8:2 and 8:11 and consider what it means to have the Spirit of the living God at work inside you! The law of the Spirit of life in Christ Jesus defies our earthbound nature. You are free, cleansed, and purified in Christ Jesus.

a. Write out a prayer of thanks for your purity, freedom, and calling because of Christ's finished work on the cross (even if this reality doesn't feel true to you *yet*).

7. Read Colossians 3:4 and consider that when Christ appears, you won't be exposed for all of the things you've done; you'll be vindicated for choosing to follow Christ. Write out a prayer asking God to help you live from an eternal perspective.

⌒ DISCUSSION STARTERS ⌒

1. What kinds of scenarios in your life most stir up the voice of condemnation in your head?

2. What's your typical response during such times?

3. Can you think of a time when you stood strong against the lies of the enemy? What did you do and how did it turn out?

4. What are some steps you can take to live a condemnation-free life with a strong sense of your identity in Christ?

5. What advice do you have for the woman who lives under the constant cloud of condemnation? What are some practical steps she could take?

6. What's the best way to cultivate a listening ear to hear God's voice and the faith to silence the enemy's voice?

Section Four

Believe
God's Word

Every word
I've spoken to you
will come true on time—
God's time.

Luke 1:20 THE MESSAGE

7

Follow
His Lead

The Lord is my shepherd; I have all that I need.

Psalm 23:1 NLT

Sometimes people are reluctant to do more for God. They feel stretched beyond their limits as it is. But anyone willing to break through their fears will discover that life is best and most satisfying when we're living God's adventure.[1]

—Bruce Wilkinson

Several years ago I showed up at a retreat with the wrong speaking notes. As soon as I walked into the main hall, I noticed decorations and brochures adorned with seeds, old trees, and fresh sprouts, clearly displaying a "Rooted and Grounded in Christ" theme. My heart sunk to my toes. I had prepared for a "Deep Waters" theme. How did I mess this up?

Without boring you with too much detail, I had about twenty retreats booked that year, and several back-to-back retreats at the time. My contacts for both weekends had the same first name and both signed their emails with their first names. Somewhere along the line, my emails from the other contact ended up in this weekend's event file. That's never happened before and it hasn't happened since.

When the leaders came into the sanctuary, I dropped to my knees and begged forgiveness. "You'll never believe what I've done," I said, and proceeded to explain my blunder. Thankfully they pulled me up, wrapped their arms around me, and said, "Bring the message God has given you! We want to hear it." Bless God for such wonderful women!

I dug deep, prayed hard, and appealed to God to bless these women in spite of me. My misstep compelled me to engage my faith on a whole new level. I felt a bit like the wedding hosts at Cana in Galilee, embarrassed because they ran out of wine. If Jesus didn't show up and turn my water message into wine, I—like the Cana wedding hosts—feared I'd look like an unprepared fool.[2]

We had a tremendous weekend. God brought great strength and boldness to my messages. He miraculously healed a woman's back after years of painful struggle. Women intimately encountered God and recommitted their lives to Him. God's power at work simply awed me, especially since I prepared for the wrong retreat. I delivered a "deep waters" message surrounded by seeds, trees, plant decorations, and God's grace.

God moves powerfully through us when we make our imperfect selves available to Him. When we finally get to the place where we truly believe God has a plan for our lives and we're willing to walk through the fire to lay hold of it, the Shepherd leads us into territory where we see His plan begin to unfold.

Time and time again we'll find ourselves in situations where the need in front of us is greater than our supply or the task before us far exceeds our ability. This is where God's purposes *for us* and His promises *to us* converge.

He prepares and positions us for His purposes every moment of every hour. Every experience we have matters to Him. Since He's always at work, may we ever be attentive to the Lord. May we walk this faith journey with eyes wide open, ears attuned to His voice, and a heart that fully trusts our Shepherd.

With every detail of our lives accounted for, Jesus writes a beautiful story that's bigger than we are, one that echoes into eternity. Since Jesus cherishes our steps and counts the hairs on our head, may we live fully alive, fully aware at the wonder of it all.

Do You Trust Him?

For many years I longed for God to call me out of my comfortable cul-de-sac and use me in significant unlike-me ways. Yet other times, like a scaredy-cat, I preferred to cut and run and hide when things got too close and personal for my taste.

Like the apostle Peter, I loved Jesus and my heart beat wildly for Him. But when given the option of looking at the wind of my fears or looking at Jesus, my fears often won the day. It's hard to step out of the boat when you're anchored to your fears.

I remember a time when I said too much. I shared my story on the first night of a women's retreat. I felt comfortable with these women, but I barely knew them, and I gave more details of my story than I usually do. I revealed a fear-battle I hadn't won yet, and then spoke of God's faithfulness, abundant grace, and unending love. I shared of His promise to never leave us.

Even so, I left the stage feeling exposed and completely unqualified to be one of God's messengers.

The next morning a woman approached me with tear-stained eyes. She shared how she connected with Jesus during my message. She gently touched my arm and said, "Thank you for being so real with us last night. God used you profoundly, and He spoke to me deeply. Thank you."

Later that day, another woman approached me. She kept a safe distance, awkwardly tilted her head, and said, "Wow. You sure give a lot of yourself away. Don't you ever get paranoid that women are just going to talk about you and pick apart your story?"

Yes, I do, I thought to myself. But to her I said, "I entrust myself to God. He's my defender. He'll take care of me." And though my answer was biblical and true, I still wanted to go to my room, put my head under the pillow, and consider a new line of service—one that allowed me to save face and keep people at a safe distance. Wow, two such different responses to the same sincere offering. No wonder it's scary to step out and trust God with our dreams and desires.

Thankfully I've learned that I'm not the only woman who wrestles with this inner conflict.

Use me.

No, don't.

Yes, do.

Why are You using her more than You use me?

Bless Your heart, God! Will You help me make up my mind?

Deep within our souls there's a sincere desire for God to use us, a desire imparted to us from God Himself. Woven into our spiritual DNA is a beautiful calling and divine purpose for us to fulfill.

But tangled up within are also selfish roots that wrap themselves around the budding dream within us, and if we don't deal with them, they diminish the power and purity of God's call on our lives. Our mixed motives will compel us to hide when we should stand up and step out, and our ambitions may compel us to run ahead when obedience calls us to pause and wait.

We'll trip over ourselves more often than not if we refuse to allow God to purify and sanctify our desires. That's why those times of refining are so important. They reveal the self-stuff in us that has to go, and they strengthen the God-stuff within us necessary to walk out our call.

Two of the most common "self" roots are self-promotion and self-preservation. We love to dream with God about His desires for us. But as soon as we start to dream, impatience kicks in. Our selfishness loves a good shortcut and revels in the limelight. Once we identify a certain desire, we want its fulfillment yesterday. Or at least sometime this week. We compare ourselves to others and suddenly notice how far along they are in the journey.

When we finally put these self-sins in their place, we have to contend with the fears that compel us to self-preserve and self-protect. When God calls us up, it's easy and tempting to look down at everything we lack. We feel the limitations of our humanity and we become acutely aware of our weaknesses and foibles. Sometimes, the closer we get to laying hold of our calling, the more we tend to think to ourselves, *I could really mess this up.*

When we focus on our fears, the risk of stepping out feels greater than the potential reward of living by faith. Daring to dream is no small thing. And it's not for the faint of heart. But in Christ we're called, appointed, and equipped to live lives bigger than we are.

Can you and I win the inner battle that keeps us from living out God's highest and best purposes for us? We can and we will, if we trust more in God's supply than in our lack, in His strength than in our weakness, and in His ability than in our inability. We've got nothing to offer apart from the Lord. But *with* Him, victory is ours for sure.

But first, we need to stop judging ourselves by what we lack. We come alive, find courage, and gain ground, to the extent that we keep our eyes on the One who says we lack no good thing and who qualifies us as we go. Do you trust Him?

God's Supernatural Supply

It always amazes me how graciously God meets us amidst our messes and how He fills in the gaps where we lack. The other day I found an insight in the gospel of Matthew that startled me. Jesus just faced off with the Pharisees and Sadducees (who, by the way, hated each other but came together because of their mutual disdain for the Savior). These guys demanded a sign, a miracle to prove His deity. Jesus had nothing to prove to them and had no intention of accommodating their prideful unbelief. Even so, the face-off with the religious leaders stirred up Jesus' love and concern for His closest friends, the disciples.

Once the disciples got in the boat and pushed off shore, they realized they'd forgotten the bread. Jesus, still mulling over His conversation with the Pharisees and Sadducees, cautioned the disciples to guard against the leaven of the Pharisees and Sadducees.

I know myself so well. I would have responded the way the disciples did. Here's their basic response: "We forgot the bread. He's talking about the bread. He's mad that we forgot the bread. How could we forget the bread?"

Can you just picture Jesus breathing a heavy sigh and saying, "Really? You think this is about the bread? Weren't you with Me when I multiplied the loaves and fishes and fed thousands *both* times? Do you really think your little mishap will ruin our day? I've got lunch! What I'm saying is, guard your heart!"

Now, let's apply this to us: Jesus calls us to guard our hearts and minds. He invites us to walk intimately with Him, that we might see Him, know Him, and love Him more with each passing day.

We simply cannot add to what He's already done. He saves us by His grace. He calls us by His grace. He give us a purpose in life, not because He needs us, but because He loves us. We're privileged to even be associated with the Creator.

Anything we do from here is in grateful *response* to His amazing love. We can't jump high enough, run far enough, or give enough away to add to His finished work on our behalf.

And praise God, when we trip up, forget the bread, miss the date, or prepare for the wrong event, His sufficiency more than makes up for our insufficiency. In fact, it's in our weak places where His glory shines brightest. We don't take God by surprise when we mess up. He's already made provision for us. The depths of His love for us, the understanding of our need for Him, go far beyond what we can comprehend. Such amazing love.

This is not to say we won't at times have to bear the consequences for our wrong choices and missteps, but it is to say that God is able to make all things work together for the good for those who love Him and are called according to His purpose (see Romans 8:28).

Jesus says to guard against the influences of legalism and worldliness. These two points must be on the forefront of our minds:

∾ Our efforts cannot save us.

∾ The influences of the world *can* derail us (if we're not careful).

But regarding perfection and performance, we won't always do it all right. We'll fall, we'll fail, and we'll trip over ourselves at times. Thankfully, Jesus cherishes us every bit as much when we miss the mark. Scripture clearly says that God's power is perfected in our weakness and that His Spirit is at work within us to make us more like Him (see 2 Corinthians 12:9).

We're just not going to be able to do it right all of the time. We'll make mistakes, embarrass ourselves, forget the words, and forget the bread on occasion. What God absolutely loves, what He cannot get enough of, is a humble heart full of faith (instead of an anxious heart full of fear). He draws near to the humble. He's deeply pleased by a faith that trusts *Him* more than we trust ourselves. God's supply is our supply.

We Are Kept by the Power of God

Maybe you don't relate to the unreasonable fear of exposure I wrote about in chapter 4, but yours is a fear of failure, rejection, or even discomfort. The enemy knows which threats or taunts will impact us most, and he'll poke at those fears and stir up our insecurities. Anything to take our eyes off God. Scripture says the enemy prowls around like a roaring lion, an adversary, looking for a weakness or vulnerability in our lives (see 1 Peter 5:8–9). Have you noticed how he pokes at the same old places again and again?

Sometimes it seems we'll never get free of his harassment. The truth is, until we see Jesus face-to-face, we'll be subject to the enemy's attempts to derail us. But that doesn't mean he'll succeed. Remember, victory is ours, not his!

If we entrust ourselves to the Most High God, if Jesus is our Lord and Savior, then the promise of grace and peace *in abundance* is ours! And God Himself promises to keep us by His power. We "who are *kept* by the power of God through faith . . ." will triumph over our fears (1 Peter 1:5 NKJV, emphasis mine).

As Warren Wiersbe shares, "The word translated 'kept' in the verse above is a military word that means guarded and shielded. The tense of the verb reveals that we are *constantly* being guarded by God, assuring us that we shall safely arrive in heaven."[3]

One of the beautiful things about following the Shepherd is this: He's always with us, stirring within us a desire to know Him more, awakening within us a heart to trust Him more, and creating within us a greater hunger for His Word. We grow as we go. And we simply follow His lead. In his book *You Were Made for More,* Jim Cymbala writes:

As you give yourself to God's special assignment, you will pray more and with a deeper sense of passion. You will hunger for a greater understanding of the Bible and how it applies to your life. You will regularly sense the help of the Holy Spirit, since God always works *with* those who give themselves to work *for* him.[4]

Called to Go Beyond What We Know

My friend and pastor Mark Spencer used the following diagram in a sermon one day, and I loved the visual so much that I asked him if I could borrow it. Look at this first circle as your comfort zone, or your known zone:

We are the queens of our comfort zone. We love this known zone! We know our way around here. We have all kinds of things to prop us up here. My favorite pillow, my morning coffee, and my fireplace adorn my comfort zone. The familiar highways I take to work every day are well within my comfort zone. Certain friends that I know and love are a part of what makes my known zone a wonderful, safe place to be.

The sweet things that make our life comfortable are gifts from God. Routine and everydayness brings stability and consistency to life. Responsibility is a good thing. But here's a critical point every believer must remember: Our routines and comforts can just as quickly become idols if we allow them to insulate us from taking risks, from giving sacrificially, and from trusting God. We're all called to some kind of daily grind. But when we get so caught up in the repetition of our days that we forget to look for God, we miss out on His invitations to step out and step up in ways that take us beyond what we know.

How about you? What parts of your life prop you up and cocoon you from trusting God for a life of greater significance?

One thing that's attractive about our comfort zone is this: We're a big deal in our comfort zone. It's a world we can control to some extent. We like it that way.

The problem is, if we live in the comfort zone and make accommodations for self-preservation, that zone begins to shrink. Even what we know begins to diminish. For example, if you spend every evening and every weekend watching TV instead of engaging with others, exercising your body, or reading something that challenges you, while it may be the easier thing to do and you might be comfortable, you'll lose ground in a hurry.

Not to say that God doesn't grant us nights snuggled up in front of a good movie. But most of us have an inner sense of when we cross the line from having our comforts serve us to where we find ourselves continually serving our comforts and making accommodations for them in a way that makes us soft and selfish.

It takes initiative to engage in life, to do the important things. God wired us for forward movement. He calls us to go from strength to strength, glory to glory, shining ever brighter until the full light of day. By orders of the King, we're assigned to a life of significance, one that involves faith and answered prayers, mountains and valleys, dreams and heart's desires, and loving and ministering to others.

None of these can happen if we prefer comfort over significance, or ease over engagement. Oftentimes we don't like to leave the known zone because we'd rather save face than take a faith risk. But the Bible says if we try to save our life, we'll lose it. *"For whoever desires to save his life will lose it, but whoever loses his life for My sake will find it"* (Matthew 16:25 NKJV).

We'd be more likely to step out of our known zone and activate our faith if we understood how significantly Christ has equipped us to go to unknown places and thrive there. Rick Renner reveals a powerful truth based on John 1:12:

> "But as many as received him, to them gave he the power to become sons of God, even to them that believe on his name." This verse reveals that you received divine power the day you became a child of God. The word "power" is the Greek word "exousia." It describes *delegated authority or influence*. The day you chose to make Jesus your Lord and Savior is the day He delegated to you the power and authority to become a child of God. Think of it—at that moment of decision, all the power, authority, and divine influence that is resident within the mighty name of Jesus Christ came to live inside of you![5]

When we receive Christ as our Savior, He delegates to us a certain measure of authority and influence. When we walk in our divine authority and influence and steward what's been given us, we receive more influence from the Lord and a greater capacity for the things of God. Yet if we disregard such a high privilege and call, even the influence imparted to us will diminish.

> "Consider carefully what you hear," Jesus continued. "With the measure you use, it will be measured to you—and even more. Whoever has will be given more; whoever does not have, even what they have will be taken from them."
>
> Mark 4:24–25

We are made for growth, for transformation, and for others. If we make life about us and about our comforts, we will tragically miss our whole purpose for living on the earth today.

Even amidst our everyday lives and familiar routines are opportunities to know God's love in an increasingly powerful way. As we engage our faith in how we approach our daily duties, our children, our neighbors, or even our involvement at church, we'll learn to see God move in ways that surprise us. We'll learn to take risks in ways that no one else may notice but God.

When Kevin and I first moved into the community where we now live, we visited a few churches hoping to find a place to call home. One particular church seemed pleasant enough at first, but not one person greeted us, said hi, or made any effort to connect with us. Do I sound like a whiner yet?

After the service I slipped into the restroom, glad for the chance to get away from the clusters of people who didn't notice this newbie in their midst. Once I got into the bathroom stall, I bowed my head and lamented to the Lord, *"Father, I'm lonely. Nobody even cares that we're here. Nobody has reached out to me. It's hard going to new places."* I expected Jesus to commiserate with me and feel as sorry for me as I felt for myself. So His response surprised me: *"How long have you walked with Me?"* I whispered back, "Um, for about twenty-five years or so." He continued, *"You know Me well. That's enough. Go out there and reach out to someone who's really in need."*

Here's something you must know about me: I'm mostly an introvert by nature. Small talk with strangers is absolutely painful for me. If I can get past the surface stuff and into the depths and substance of a person's life, I'll talk with anyone. But I'd rather go to the dentist than strike up a conversation with a total stranger. It's way out of my comfort zone.

As soon as I ventured out of my bathroom safe zone and back into the church foyer, I saw her. I peered through the throng of happy church people and saw a young mom clutching her purse and standing alone against the wall, her children staying close beside her. I approached her and reached out my hand. "How are you today?" Instantly her eyes pooled with tears. She shook her head as she wrestled to formulate her words. "I've just been diagnosed with Lyme disease. I'm a young mom and don't know how I'll ever manage my life feeling the way I do."

I stood there dumbfounded. Years ago, I walked in her very shoes, battled Lyme disease with three young children. I stepped in close, grabbed her shoulders, and said, "Oh, honey, I've been there. I'm so, so sorry. Here's what I learned, and this is what I know to be true . . ." I shared practical and spiritual insights that got me through my years of Lyme disease while mothering little ones. In an instant, God connected us through our similar stories.

"Mind if I pray for you?" I asked. She answered simply, "Please do." I held her hands and lifted her needs up to the Lord. I so sensed His love for both of us, felt so glad for the opportunity to minister His love to somebody who really needed a fresh touch that day.

I prayed a prayer under my breath in that moment, *Lord, forgive me for my constant bent toward selfishness. I don't want to miss a thing You have for me. I'm here to serve You, and it's always an honor to do so.*

With her eyes still wet with tears and a new smile on her face, she asked me a surprising question. "Are you on staff here?" I laughed. "Um, no. I'm just visiting."

⁓

Remember, you and I each have a significant big-picture call on our lives, one that God appointed to us before we were born. And a central part of that appointed purpose is the *daily* call of surrender and obedience. Courageous and called women invite God to divinely interrupt our day so that we can participate in His everyday miracles. Our life purpose is to be used for His kingdom purposes.

Sometimes we get to see the significant role we play in God's story. Because we dared to step out and engage in a need, someone gets saved, or healed, or restored in some way. Maybe we have the privilege of partnering with God to deliver groceries to a family in need, or to pray with someone whose marriage is in trouble and we see God miraculously restore their marriage. Those are the times that remind us how important our obedience is in the whole scheme of things.

But other times we don't get to see the fruit of our actions. Sometimes it needs to be enough to simply respond to the inner nudge, to obey His voice, and to trust that we'll see the impact of our faith steps when we see Jesus face-to-face. Every faith step matters to God. Read this powerful passage from 2 Thessalonians 1:11–12:

> So we keep on praying for you, asking our God to enable you to live a life worthy of his call. May he give you the power to accomplish all the good things your faith prompts you to do. Then the name of our Lord Jesus will be honored because of the way you live, and you will be honored along with him. (NLT)

A living, breathing, active faith—that's our birthright and call in Christ Jesus.

And while we're called to continually look for God in the everydayness of our lives, we're also called to a life of faith that involves occasional adventures that take us beyond the known zone. Though our comforts bring us comfort, our call leads us beyond them on a regular basis. The second circle in the diagram represents the learning zone:

The learning zone is the realm just outside our comfort zone. Suppose you are a big deal in the corporate world, but then you step out of your comfortable existence to go on a mission trip. Folks who've made numerous international trips surround you.

They seem comfortable in their own skin. You, however, feel off balance, out of your element, and quite small. You're unfamiliar with this world, and it's a big one. Part of you wishes you could go back to your planet where you know your way around. You're in your learning zone.

The beautiful thing about the learning zone is this: When you follow Jesus to the unknown places He invites you to, He goes with you and stays by your side every second of every hour. He equips you to be there. And though it's humbling to feel so small, you find a new level of dependence on a God who is so very big. Over time, you find God to be faithful, you learn your way around, and guess what happens next? Your comfort zone—your known zone—expands to include new territory that once seemed unfamiliar to you. Your known zone increases and God prepares you for more new places of promise.

The final circle in the diagram represents the faith zone or, as my friend Pastor Mark Spencer affectionately calls it, "the freak-out zone"

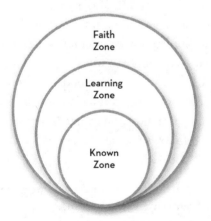

This is the realm where when you step out, if God doesn't come through for you, you will most certainly fail. It's often a scary place to be, but an exhilarating one at the same time. Since we cannot please God without faith (see Hebrews 11:6), we must be willing to follow God out of our comfort to places where we are completely and totally dependent on Him.

I've read Bruce Wilkinson's book *Beyond Jabez* several times. The author's faith in the bigness of God inspires me to trust God in ways that disrupt my comforts but stir up my faith. Read the following excerpt:

> The prayer for territory is not focused on your comfort, but on change. Whenever you ask for "more," you really are asking God to take you beyond where you have ever been before—into the unknown and unpredictable. God has an exciting adventure waiting for you, and it will involve some risks. But as you grow to know personally the God who urges you to exercise greater influence for Him, you'll soon learn that He will never abandon you.[6]

You've heard it said that God does not call the qualified, He qualifies the called. He's calling you beyond what you know so that you might *know Him* more. Are you willing to look the fool, to be in need, to face a giant, just to see how *for you* God is? His promises are yours. Living by faith means we'll sometimes be called on to speak without having all the answers, or to step out without having the full plan, or to stay back though a wide open door of opportunity seems like an obvious next step. Living by faith means we surrender our will and our logical reasoning that we might follow the Shepherd of our hearts because we trust Him more than we trust ourselves. Jesus both precedes us and follows us. He places His hand of blessing on our head (see Psalm 139:5).

> What a God we have! And how fortunate we are to have him, this Father of our Master Jesus! Because Jesus was raised from the dead, we've been given a brand-new life and have everything to live for, including a future in heaven—and the future starts now! God is keeping careful watch over us and the future. The Day is coming when you'll have it all—life healed and whole.
>
> 1 Peter 1:3–5 THE MESSAGE

Precious Lord,

I want every minute of my life to count for You. Awaken me with fresh passion, fiery faith, and a renewed resolve to follow hard after You. O Lord, bless me, indeed! Increase Your territory through me. May Your power be evident in and all around me. May Your love flow freely through me. Keep me from evil and from harm, and help me to live a life full of faith, rich in holiness. Increase my capacity to live and walk by the Spirit. Awaken Your passions within me that I might be quick to obey You. My life is in Your hands. I trust You and will follow You, Lord. Change the world through me. Amen.

⟞ STUDY QUESTIONS ⟝

1. Read Matthew 26:31–32 and answer the following questions:

    a. Imagine how Jesus felt in the hours prior to His arrest. He knew what kind of suffering awaited Him at Calvary. He needed His friends that night, yet they scattered. What are some of the reasons His friends abandoned Him that night? Really think about this one. Can you identify with any of those feelings? Explain.

    b. Read verse 32 and notice how Jesus assured His friends. What did He say to them?

2. Verse 32 is short, but it's packed with meaning. In so many words Jesus said, "I know you don't have what it takes to stand strong every minute of the day. And after I've gone to the cross to pay for your sins, after I've confronted and defeated the enemy of your soul, I will meet up with you again and infuse you with strength." When you consider

what Jesus was saying to His friends in that statement, and you consider Christ's gracious love, how does it make you feel?

3. Read Matthew 26:33 and notice Peter's response to Christ's words. Peter is sincerely passionate and more than a little self-confident. Peter, just like us, needed his passions purified, otherwise they'd trip him up again and again. Explain why self-confidence leads us into the danger zone whereas God confidence leads us into the faith zone.

4. Read Matthew 26:36–41 and answer the following questions:

   a. Jesus asked Peter, James, and John to stand watch with Him during His dark night of the soul in the garden of Gethsemane. How did they respond?

   b. Not only did Peter fall asleep when Jesus needed Him, he denied ever knowing Him. Look at verse 41 of this passage and then consider the leaven of the Pharisees and Sadducees (the influences of legalism and worldliness). What does it mean for you as a believer to watch and pray? What does that look like on a practical level?

   c. Why are watchfulness and prayerfulness so important when it comes to stepping out of your known zone?

5. Now let's look at a transformed, humbled, and empowered Peter. Read Acts 3:1–16 and answer the following questions:

   a. Did you notice any pride or self-importance surface in Peter when this man asked for Peter's help? What was Peter's initial response to the crippled man?

   b. In verse 11 we read that the people were astonished and came running to see these miracle-working men. Peter could have reveled in the moment, but he didn't.

What about Peter's response to the fascinated crowd stands out to you?

c. Notice how Peter's commitment is to truth, and no longer to fame. He had a new fire and boldness to his words. Peter's self-ambitious, self-preserving ways had died, and the Spirit of God in Peter lived strong. Write out a prayer asking God to work miracles in and through you.

6. Stepping out of our comfort zone almost always involves risk. And yet it's safer to step out when Jesus calls us than to stay back in an effort to protect ourselves. Do you remember the story of Esther from the Old Testament? (If not, definitely read the whole book of Esther. It'll challenge and inspire your faith in every way.) There's a crisis point in the story where Mordecai alerts Esther to the plot to kill the Jews, and he wants her to intercede. Read her response in Esther 4:9–11, and write her response in your own words.

a. Can you think of a time you responded to a need or a call in the same way?

7. Now read Mordecai's response in Esther 4:12–14 and answer the following questions:

a. What stands out to you in this passage regarding God's movement in the world and our participation with Him?

b. What social issues in our day concern you most? How is God intervening in these issues (who is He using)?

c. If God calls you to get involved, what do you think your instinctive response will be? (Ask God to fill you with faith so you're ready when He calls.)

～ DISCUSSION STARTERS ～

1. Describe your comfort zone.

2. What do you love about your comfort zone?

3. What convictions are stronger than your desire for comfort? What calls you out of your comfort zone?

4. Describe a time when God called you into the learning zone. How did you work through the discomfort of feeling out of your element?

5. Tell about a time when God called you way out, over your head, into the faith zone. What did you learn about the faithfulness of God?

8

Engage
Your Faith

But you, dear friends, carefully build yourselves up in this most holy faith by praying in the Holy Spirit, staying right at the center of God's love, keeping your arms open and outstretched, ready for the mercy of our Master, Jesus Christ. This is the unending life, the real life!

Jude 1:20–21 THE MESSAGE

He is the God of limitless resources—the only limit comes from us. Our requests, our thoughts, and our prayers are too small, and our expectations are too low. God is trying to raise our vision to a higher level, call us to have greater expectations, and thereby bring us to greater appropriation.[1]

—A. B. Simpson

We're nearing the fifteenth anniversary of my husband's battle with cancer. Now that we're on the other side, Kevin is more present in the moment. He's more deeply engaged in the things of God. And he's more intent on living a life that really matters. Though we pray we don't have to go the cancer route again, we hold fast to the treasures we picked up on that journey.

Kevin stands a sturdy six foot three and weighs over 250 pounds, but major surgery showed him just how fragile he really is. He has an amazing capacity to oversee the construction of large-scale projects, but when sickness wrapped him in a blanket and put him in a chair all day, Kevin learned on a deeper level that every breath, every movement, even his best skills are gifts from above. As I mentioned earlier, Kevin tends toward workaholism, but radiation taught him how to cease striving and know that *God* is indeed God (see Psalm 46:10).

Kevin used to pride himself on how much he could get done in a day. Now he daily humbles himself and acknowledges he can do no good thing apart from God. I loved the man I married before he had cancer. I treasure the man he is now. That painful season woke up his soul and now he's fully engaged in kingdom life.

During the weeks Kevin went through radiation treatments, he spent a lot of time sleeping in his chair. When the neighborhood kids knocked at the door and invited my sons out to play, my boys usually replied, "No thanks. We want to stay in with our dad."

While Kevin slept in his recliner, the boys sat quietly on the floor next to his chair. They played video games, or trucks, or whatever else interested them at the moment. They seemed to feel most settled and safe when they stayed close to their dad.

One day a friend brought over a nice meal for us and some special treats for the boys. All three of our sons sat in a row on the floor next to their dad's chair fully focused on their game, completely unaware of the gift they just received.

I thanked my friend over and over again for her thoughtfulness. I explained to the boys what nice treats she brought for them. But clearly, they didn't hear me. Then I said, "Boys, what do you say?"

On cue, they turned their heads and—without any sincerity whatsoever—they spouted, "Sooorrrry!" And just as quickly turned back to play their game.

Embarrassed, I chuckled under my breath and said, "Um. Sorry. Wrong programmed response." Awkward. Though they were mostly present with their dad, my boys missed the significance of the moment.

Thankfully, when we nestle up close to our heavenly Father, we're less apt to be so out of touch with the moment. When we stay close to the heart of God, our heart will beat in rhythm with His and our words will line up more consistently with our hearts. As we walk in the Lord's presence, we grow more aware of the divine moments on earth.

No Autopilot Christianity

The extent to which we dare to move into new territory with Jesus is the extent we realize how much we need Him. And the longer we walk with Jesus, the more we learn to trust Him. Every serious follower of Christ eventually learns that though Jesus is utterly committed to us and completely faithful to lead us into glory, He's not too concerned with our immediate desire for comfort.

Mostly, Jesus cares about our eternal impact, because how we live or don't live today resonates with us into eternity. He teaches us to love and serve Him well on earth so we can reign with and worship Him in heaven.

Our human tendency, though, is to miss the divine opportunities in our midst and instead address the symptoms of our present moments. When we're uncomfortable, we like to medicate. When we're afraid, we opt for running away. When we're discontent, we like to consume. When we're rattled by somebody else's pain, we're apt to explain it away so we don't have to get involved.

God's tendency, on the other hand, is to deeply involve us in the opportunity of the present moment, to help us see potential in our need, power in our prayers, and possibility in our impossibilities. As we engage with Him, He sets eternity in our hearts. He teaches us to redeem the moments so they'll count for eternity.

Cruise-control Christianity drives us to *get through* each moment, causing us to completely miss its divine significance. Part of what it means to live a life of promise and impossibilities is simply to scoop the present moment in our hands and lift it up to God. This means we take our foot off the gas on occasion, we pull over to the side of the road, roll down the window, and we let the sun warm our face. We remember that the whole earth is the Lord's, *and everything in it* (see Psalm 24:1).

Every time we—like the boy who surrendered his lunch—give Jesus what we have in our hand, divine and eternal influence takes place. We *must* be fully present with the Lord in our everyday circumstances because *our present moments are only valuable to the extent that we eternally invest them.*

God knows what we need more than we know what we need. He makes us run when we need greater endurance. He leads us beside still waters when we need rest. When spiritual coasting sounds like a wonderful option, yet we really need spiritual conditioning, He leads us to a steep mountain and teaches us how to engage our faith-muscles. And He imparts fresh vision to us when we lose perspective in the valley.

When our own legs threaten to give out, Jesus picks us up and carries us or He teaches us how to keep walking and to find our strength in Him. This is important because it's only in *His* strength that we can accomplish the impossible.

The problem is, if we stop looking for God in our daily lives, if we stop seeking after Him and listening for Him, we subtly move from a living, breathing fellowship with Him to a rote and wooden walk apart from Him.

Engaging With God in the Present Moment

Without God's constant influence in our lives, it's all too easy to loosen our grip of faith and to trust our own footing more. When we rely on yesterday's laurels to help us navigate through today's trials, we become autopilot Christians.

Have you ever found yourself going through the motions in your prayers? Saying one thing while thinking about another? I know I have. I have so much Scripture stored up in my soul from years of praying God's Word, I can instinctively pray Scripture with my mouth and run through my grocery list in my mind. And this is not a virtue!

Jesus said, "People honor me with their lips, but their hearts are far from me" (Matthew 15:8). Exactly. When I catch myself saying one thing and thinking another, I know it's time to reengage my faith. I've learned that when I grab hold of my present concerns, wrap my arms around the present moment, and bring my whole self into the presence of God, power, insight, and revelation return to my soul.

Have you endured a spiritual season where it occurred to you that you've not once intentionally engaged your faith or listened for the voice of God? The solution is delightfully and wonderfully simple. Look to the Lord and His strength and trust that He's just a prayer away.

Try something for me. Extend your arm out to your side so it's parallel with the ground, palm up. Now bend at the elbow several times, touch your shoulder, and extend your arm out again. From a fitness perspective, that motion is considered movement, but not engagement. Now extend your arm out again, but this time make a fist and concentrate on your bicep (the muscle that bulges when you flex), then slowly flex that muscle. Notice how

141

you have to engage the muscle in order to flex it. That's the difference between movement and engagement.

I might be moving my mouth with all of the right words, I might be busily serving at church with all of the right methods, but the scary thing is, I can look the part of the Christ-follower and miss the heart of Christ amidst all of my action.

Maybe you've been on the receiving end of someone else's autopilot, disengaged response. Do you remember what that felt like? Perhaps that person received a fresh truth from God about a similar situation years ago but have since stopped seeking Him for fresh revelations and insight for the *now* and *present* moments. All they had to offer you was a stale piece of bread.

Did their offering help you to better know the Father's love or long for more time in His presence? Or did you walk away feeling like you had just chewed on sawdust or stepped in gum? Doesn't God offer us fresh mercies for each new day?

A dear friend of mine sings beautifully and serves alongside her husband in a worship ministry. When she sings, she looks like an angel. Her voice is the main instrument she uses to serve and worship God.

You can imagine her despair when she experienced vocal issues that kept her from singing and even talking at times. She faced the very real possibility of never singing again. She's a social butterfly and comes alive when she worships, so losing her voice felt to her like someone had sliced off her wings. Not only did she feel cut off from the ministry she and her husband had built together, she felt cut off from her friends because she wasn't able to process her pain with us.

Though people meant well, can you imagine some of the platitudes people served her?

~ *Oh, well, God won't give you more than you can handle.*

~ *Maybe your voice got too important to you.*

~ *At least you have your health.*

~ *Maybe God has a plan that doesn't involve your gifts.*

If you've been on the receiving end of religious response that lacked fresh revelation, you understand the importance of cultivating a living, breathing relationship with Christ so you can rightly represent Him to a world in need. Jesus counts on us to reflect *His-very-much-alive-heart* to the world.

We Are Ambassadors

We are ambassadors and messengers. And we serve a loving, engaged, and active God. Not that we're always going to get it right or say it right on every occasion, though. Moses stammered and stuttered, but he enjoyed close fellowship with God. The result? God considered Moses a friend (see Exodus 33:11). And He used Moses to change the world. Our calling isn't to eloquence or perfection. But our calling *is* to faith—engaged, living, and breathing faith that pursues the heart of God and brings life to the circumstances we encounter on the journey.

Read the book of Job and consider Job's friends. If you take their statements out of the context of Job's circumstances, his friends spoke a lot of truth. But within the context of Job's trial (in which God Himself was writing history), Job's friends missed the mark completely. Their offerings lacked love and came out sounding like one big, long "You know what your problem is . . . *it's you*" statement.

What was God's response to their "truthful" insights? God told Job that his friends did not speak correctly about Him. They relied so heavily on their long acquired wisdom that they utterly missed God's perfect heart in Job's present circumstances.

Job's friends offered platitudes and packaged answers to a man who desperately needed to hear from God. Their lack of fresh and loving revelation only enhanced Job's suffering.

If we are serious about living the life God promised us, we need to be serious about intentionally seeking hard after God Himself. If you're in a season of life where you honestly can't remember the last time you heard from God or experienced a sense of His abiding presence, do not rest until you've made time and space in your life to get alone with God.

Though forward-moving faith calls for times of rest and replenishment, it never involves autopilot, coasting-so-I-don't-have-to-think-about-it Christianity. Spiritual traction cannot happen apart from an intimate and intentionally engaged walk with Jesus.

Whatever God showed us last year, or even yesterday, He has something better, something deeper, and something more profound to show us today. He intends that we go from strength to strength, glory to glory, shining ever brighter until the full light of day (see Proverbs 4:18).

Though we treasure past wisdom gained through victory and trial, we must never stop seeking hard after God today.

May we walk intimately with God and thus become reliable messengers of His engaged presence and profound love. As Proverbs 13:17 says, "An unreliable messenger stumbles into trouble, but a reliable messenger brings healing" (NLT).

Strength Through Faith

As a former fitness professional, I noticed two types of people who *faithfully* showed up to the health club to work out month in and month out: those who never got stronger, whose bodies never changed; and those who progressively got more fit and who grew stronger with each passing month.

How is it possible to faithfully and consistently work out, week after week, month after month, and yet barely have anything to show for it? Let me ask a similar question: How is it possible to faithfully and consistently attend church week after week, year after year, and experience almost no growth to speak of?

Churches are filled with sincere Christians who consistently attend church, volunteer in the nursery, and bake pies for the church potluck. From a distance, they look the part. But when you scoot up close, you find them to have the same addictive tendencies, or proneness to anger, or propulsion to gossip as some of the unsaved folks you know. And year after year, nothing changes in their character. Have you ever wondered why that is?

Of course that's a complicated question requiring a multifaceted answer. But the most basic answer is this: engagement. It's just not enough to go through the motions. Movement doesn't change us, soul engagement does. Ephesians 3:20 is one of my favorite verses in the Bible because it speaks of two extremely important aspects of the life God offers us:

- ∽ Allowing God to work wonders through us that are totally disproportionate to who we are (*above and beyond all we could ever dare to ask or think*).

- ∽ Allowing God first to work wonders *in us,* a transformation we could never achieve on our own (*according to His mighty work within us*).

With these two points in mind, read Ephesians 3:20 with fresh eyes:

> Now to him who is able to do immeasurably more than all we ask or imagine, according to his power that is at work within us.

God's work through us is directly proportionate to His work within us. And He'll only work in us to the extent that we give Him access to our soul and permission to change us. Either we humble ourselves, admit our daily need for more of His life and influence within us (and we're beautifully changed in the process), or we continue to show up at church, look the part, and miss out on the absolute miracle of life transformation.

Just as all of our striving cannot save us, all of our serving cannot remake us. Christ in us is our hope of glory. We serve, live, give, and attempt the impossible because Jesus has done the same *for us and in us*. Everything we do is in response to the life-giving power of God mightily at work within us.

Private Prayer—Public Strength

Years ago, while waiting at the gate to catch a plane, I fumbled through my bag to find the novel I planned on reading cover to cover on my way home. Poking a hole in my self-protective bubble, a man across the aisle struck up a conversation with me. I so wanted to rest and bury my head in my novel, but I sensed that God put this man in my path to teach me something new.

The man handed me a book written by a friend of his. After some back-and-forth introductions, he said, "I don't know where you want to end up in life, but life's always about stretching and growing. If you want to get where you want to go, you can't do what you've always done. Sometimes you have to reassess your disciplines and habits, sometimes you need to fine-tune your life, and it's those small changes that end up making the biggest difference in the long run."

Though this guy didn't seem to be a man of faith (and I did share my faith with him), he gave me something very important to think about.

Instead of reading my novel on the way home, I read the book I received from this bold stranger in the airport. Here's my paraphrase of the book *The Slight Edge: Secret to a Successful Life* by Jeff Olson: Over time, your choices either promote you or expose you. What we do in secret from day to day seems of little consequence, but in due time those small hidden choices either reveal a life of discipline or sloth.

Either our teeth fall out, or they grow whiter; either our relationships break apart or they emerge stronger; either our finances fritter away or they come together; either we gain weight or we lose it.[2]

And to make a spiritual application to this same principle: Either we grow in our faith and become more intimate with God, or we fall away from Him. How we live our lives privately eventually comes out publicly. We must dare to ask ourselves, *Where's my focus? What do I replay in my head? His promises or my problems? Is my mind drawn to sin's enticement, or the promise of God's reinforcement?* As we play our thoughts forward, do they take us where we want to go? Our internal process will eventually become our external reality.

George Mueller is a faith hero whose private life involved intimate times with the Lord. As a result, he accomplished the impossible in his public life—caring for, feeding, and educating thousands of orphans over the course of his lifetime. Mueller's private life deeply impacted his public encounters.

A number of years ago I went to America with a steamship captain who was a very devoted Christian. When we were off the coast of Newfoundland, he said to me, "The last time I sailed here, which was five weeks ago, something happened that revolutionized my entire Christian life. I had been on the bridge for twenty-four straight hours when George Mueller of Bristol, England, who was a passenger on board, came to me and said, 'Captain, I need to tell you that I must be in Quebec on Saturday afternoon.' 'That is impossible,' I replied.

"'Very well,' Mueller responded, 'if your ship cannot take me, God will find some other way, for I have never missed an engagement in fifty-seven years. Let's go down to the chartroom to pray.' I looked at this man of God and thought to myself, *What lunatic asylum did he escape from?* I had never encountered someone like this. 'Mr. Mueller,' I said, 'do you realize how dense the fog is?'

"'No,' he replied, 'my eye is not on the dense fog but on the living God, who controls every circumstance of my life.'

"He then knelt down and prayed one of the most simple prayers I have ever heard. When he had finished, I started to pray, but he put his hand on my shoulder and told me *not* to pray. He said, 'First, you do not believe God will answer, and second *I believe He has.* Consequently, there is no need whatsoever for you to pray about it.'

"As I looked at him he said, 'Captain, I have known my Lord for fifty-seven years, and there has never been a single day that I have failed to get an audience with the King. Get up, Captain, and open the door, and you will see that the fog is gone.' I got up, and indeed the fog was gone. And on Saturday afternoon George Mueller was in Quebec for his meeting."[3]

Oh, to have such faith! This kind of faith isn't born out of straining, striving, and hoping really hard that God will do what He says. Proverbs 9:10 reminds us that by simply *knowing* the Holy One, we'll begin to understand Him. The more we spend time with Jesus, the more we'll get to know His character and understand His ways. He is a man of His word, a keeper of His promises. And, He rewards those who earnestly seek after Him (see Hebrews 11:6). He draws us to Himself, and then He blesses us for responding to His call.

Read this verse from Matthew 6:6: "But when you pray, go into your room, close the door and pray to your Father, who is unseen. Then your Father, who sees what is done in secret, will reward you." Private, prayerful times with the Father mark our lives with true kingdom power (see also 1 Corinthians 4:20). To know the Lord is to walk intimately with Him.

Before we even begin to pray, may we pause long enough to consider who it is we're praying to; may we marvel that He's not only given us access to His throne, He invites us to come confidently and be assured of His glad welcome (see Ephesians 3:12). When we stand in awe at the wonder of it all, our prayer times will feel like we're breathing fresh air.

And when we breathe in the fresh air of God's presence and provision, His love makes our heart beat in rhythm with His.

His power energizes to do the things He's appointed us to do. We more clearly see what in our schedule is an un-appointed, unanointed work, and we seek to align our lives with God's best purposes for us. When we're intentionally engaged with God, we're more fully engaged in the work He's assigned to us.

Whatever your calling and wherever you are in the process, may you faithfully steward what He has put in your hand. Are you called to sing? Sing with your whole heart and soul. Are you called to teach? Teach as though you're speaking the very words of God. Called to encourage? Look for and pray for divine opportunities to build others up in their faith. For the sake of His glory and your delight, engage in life with your whole heart.

Read this passage from 1 Peter 4:10–11:

> Each of you should use whatever gift you have received to serve others, as faithful stewards of God's grace in its various forms. If anyone speaks, they should do so as one who speaks the very words of God. If anyone serves, they should do so with the strength God provides, so that in all things God may be praised through Jesus Christ. To him be the glory and the power for ever and ever. Amen.

May we grow to love what Jesus loves, hate what He hates, want what He wants, do what He does, and say what He says. May we live this life fully engaged with the Spirit of God mightily at work within us.

One Sunday morning a while back, I showed up at church completely spent after a full weekend of ministry. I felt like a used-up, wrinkly dishrag that somebody had twisted dry. I didn't have a drop of moisture in my soul. To be honest, I didn't want to talk with anyone, let alone pray with anyone. I really just wanted to stay home and pull the covers over my head. But I sensed the inner nudge to go to church and trusted God would give me what I needed.

I showed up ready to *receive* what I needed, not at all prepared to give. Anything. My empty cup needed filling. Unfortunately, the service seemed boring that day (it was probably me). I felt only disappointment. Regretted that I didn't stay in bed.

After the service, an acquaintance approached me and asked if I'd pray for her friend. I'd spent the last two days at a women's retreat speaking to and praying for hundreds of women. Even my voice felt dry and cracked from fatigue.

Exhausted at the thought of giving more of myself away, I felt tempted to pray a surface prayer (that lacked engagement) so I could hightail it out to the car before anybody else needed anything more from me.

Yet as soon as I put my hands on this woman's shoulders and looked into her tormented eyes, I whispered a prayer in the depths of my soul, *Forgive me, Lord. In my weakness, I am strong in You. Wisdom for this weary soul, I pray. Wisdom and power, please. Amen.*

And then I began to pray for this dear anguished woman. Somehow, by the grace and faithfulness of *God,* He made my prayers potent with power. God supplied wisdom and revelation and even a depth of insight into parts of this woman's story that she hadn't revealed to me. This precious desperate woman wrapped her arms around me and hugged me tight. I hugged her back just as tight and marveled at the living, loving power of God. He works mightily in and through us regardless of what we think we have to offer.

Growing in the Lord is not complicated. We don't have to be theologians to be mighty in God. We just need to be present with Him. Engaged in His purposes for us. Flexible with our plans. Receptive to His divine interruptions. He invites us to walk in His presence as we live here on earth (see Psalm 116:9). When we walk intimately with the Savior, we'll have purpose in every step and we'll get where we need to go.

I listen carefully to what God the Lord is saying, for he speaks peace to his faithful people. But let them not return to their foolish ways.

Psalm 85:8 NLT

Precious Lord,

Forgive me for the countless times I've gone through the motions without engaging my heart. Awaken me again to the preciousness and power of Your presence. Draw me close to You and rekindle my prayer life once again. Lift my chin that I may look up and see the wonders of Your love. Fill me to overflowing with a renewed sense of joy and hopefulness that I may view life from Your perspective. May I be so in step and in tune with You that when others encounter me, may they encounter You. Amen.

STUDY QUESTIONS

1. Prayerfully read Proverbs 2:1–11 all the way through and consider all of the descriptive words that call for your engagement with God's Word, His wisdom, and His ways. Write down a few that stand out to you.

2. Read verses 1–2 again and journal some of your own practical ways to apply these verses in your life. Consider the following questions related to verses 1–2:

   a. How will you accept these words? Will you be teachable even when the Word of God doesn't suit you?

   b. How will you store them in your heart? What's your plan?

   c. Who will you turn to for wisdom? Do you have somebody in mind?

d. In what new discipline can you engage in order to apply your heart to understanding?

3. Read verses 3–4 and try two things during your private prayer time: Pray out loud with more passion than you ever have (engage passionate faith with your prayers), and write out an equally passionate prayer, calling on God for a greater understanding of His ways, His heart, and His influence in your life.

4. Read verse 5 and explain (after all of our pursuing, crying out, and calling on God to know Him more) why the fear of the Lord and the knowledge of Him are valuable treasures to us (hint: See Proverbs 1:7; Proverbs 9:10).

5. Read verses 7–11 and write down the benefits and blessings for those who walk with the Lord.

a. Describe in one sentence how each of these benefits will impact you personally (Victory: I win the battle over my fears; Shield: I'll trust God to protect me, etc.).

6. Read Psalm 42:1–2 and answer the following questions:

a. How would you describe your soul engagement as you read those verses? (e.g., disconnected, mostly present, fully engaged)

b. Read the passage again, out loud, and this time engage in this prayer with your heart, soul, and strength.

c. Where do you best connect with God?

d. What adjustments do you need to make in your life to more consistently meet with God, hear from God, so you can respond to Him in your daily life?

7. Read Psalm 84:9–11 and answer the following questions:

a. In your own words, why is one day in His courts better than a thousand anywhere else?

b. What does it mean to you that the Lord is both your sun and shield? (Describe in practical terms.)

c. What does it mean to you that He bestows both favor and honor? (Describe in practical terms.)

d. A blameless walk is not a perfect walk; it's a faith walk with a heart set on following and obeying Jesus. It's a heart that fears the Lord and does what He says. Does it seem as though God is withholding good things from you? It may simply be about His timing and purposes for you. But still, dare to prayerfully ask the Lord this question: *Are there any parts of my life that are disengaged from You—out of sync with Your perfect will for me?* And then spend some time listening and responding to what He says. No good thing does He withhold from those whose hearts are blameless before Him. Stay close. Stay engaged. He'll lead you faithfully.

✒ DISCUSSION STARTERS ✒

1. How would you describe your soul engagement when it comes to the following disciplines:

   a. Worship

   b. Reading God's Word

   c. Prayer

   d. Giving

   e. Serving

2. When you consider the possibility of going through life and barely growing, barely making an impact, what kinds of feelings does it stir inside of you? Does that scenario compel you to make any changes in the way you engage in life in the days to come?

3. Describe someone who lives fully engaged in God's purposes for his/her life. What do you admire most about that person?

4. In what area of your life is God calling you to engage more purposefully with Him?

5. When you think about the moment you're ushered into eternity, and the loved ones you left behind celebrate the life you've lived, what do you want them to say about you? What kind of life and faith do you want them to remember?

Here's a great reminder as we move into greater times of study and prayer:

> The study of God's Word must be accompanied by prayer that earnestly cries out for wisdom and insight. Study alone may make a Bible scholar but prayer along with the study of God's Word allows the Holy Spirit to take that revelation and transform us into spiritual people who really know God's character and ways. Pray over verses of Scripture as you read, hungering for new wisdom, revelation, and spiritual understanding.[4]

Walk by Faith

It is God who arms me with strength, and makes my way perfect. He makes my feet like the feet of deer, and sets me on my high places. He teaches my hands to make war, so that my arms can bend a bow of bronze.

Psalm 18:32–34 NKJV

Find
High Ground

But they delight in the law of the Lord, meditating on it day and night. They are like trees planted along the riverbank, bearing fruit each season. Their leaves never wither, and they prosper in all they do.

Psalm 1:2–3 NLT

So center down. Be still. Listen with the ears of your heart. Can you hear Him? The still, small voice of God is calling you to see Jesus . . . *again*. In preparation for seeing Him face-to-face, He is calling you to an experience of personal revival. Here. Now.[1]

—Anne Graham Lotz

The door squeaks and creeks, shoes stomp snow; my husband drops his bags on the floor. *Home safe.* Both glad and mad, I roll over in bed and turn my back to him. He said he'd be home hours ago. He forgot to call. He's a godly man, a good man, a hardworking man. But sometimes still, he works too much. Most women would do anything for such a loving, patient husband. And I'm grateful he's mine. But this is our struggle: engaging and losing touch; connecting and disconnecting again; saying I love you and living I love you.

We pray together every morning and almost every night. We're strong together. We're not the people we were even a year ago. We're more focused on the things of God than we've ever been.

Even so, the night frustrated me. My dad passed away two weeks ago and I still reeled from the suddenness of it all. The ache in my soul made my throat hurt.

My hubby's been loving and supportive. But I thought he'd be home that night. Second night that week I sat home alone wishing for comfort. He came home hours late and I went to bed.

Curled up in a ball, I hugged my pillow when the Lord whispered to my heart, "What did you want that you didn't receive from him?" I pressed my lips to my pillow and whispered under my breath, "Engagement."

God whispered back, "So your sin of disengagement is okay? Is this the highest ground you can find?" *No. Far from it.*

I killed the potential for a moment of joy in my sorrow. I even interrupted growth in my marriage by my earthbound response. *God, forgive me.*

This morning Kevin and I apologized. He, for forgetting . . . me, for closing up to him. Yet we both found God's hand open to us in that sacred space of repentance. Jesus offered us fresh mercy and grace as we bowed our heads and asked Him to fill us *once again.* The Lord went ahead of us as He always does and made provision for our weaknesses. Just today I read these words from my friend Ann Voskamp:

> Joy is a flame that glimmers only in the palm of the open and humble hand. In an open and humble palm, released and sur-rendered to receive, light dances, flickers happy. The moment the hand is clenched tight, fingers all pointing toward self, and

rights and demands, joy is snuffed out. Anger is the lid that suffocates joy until she lies limp and lifeless.[2]

A fist clenched tight. Just like me on the bed. When I could have had life in that moment, could have strengthened love. But I chose to honor my emotions at the expense of my marriage. Instead of rising above my feelings and seeking the higher ground of godly virtue, I chose the lower road of selfish reaction.

I've walked through many trying seasons, all of which have prepared me and trained me for where I walk now. I can see how God used the elements of my storms to strengthen me for His purposes. I marvel at the life transformation God has accomplished in my life as a result. My unholy reactions are more rare now than they've ever been. Giving God access to my soul has transformed my character, toughened my resolve, and tenderized my heart.

Still, those selfish reactions live in me. I give sin a pulse when I honor my right to it and give it room to breathe.

In every season, hidden in every choice, in every step, and in every moment, is the potential for nourishment or poison, for life or death. Hard as it is to face, and though we hate the thought of it, sometimes, for whatever reason, we'll step off of God's nourishing path and plop our foot right down in the mud and mess of our own humanity. And we'll wish we hadn't. What are we to do when we find ourselves covered with evidences of our old self, our old life?

We plop our feet in the basin and ask Jesus to wash away our mess. We humble ourselves and ask Him to forgive us our sins and cleanse us from all unrighteousness (see 1 John 1:9). We rise up from our repentance both consecrated and clean, in the full assurance that we are forgiven and free. We remember again that there is now no condemnation for those who are in Christ Jesus (see Romans 8:1). We wrap our hearts around the promise that we've been made new. We're not an improved version of our former selves; we are something different altogether.

As we move forward in our faith journey, we'll walk through seasons that try our faith and threaten our footing. We'll trip and fall and sometimes miss the high road. And in it all, we do well to remember that mercies await us at every turn. Forgiveness is ours for the asking.

And yet. *And yet,* we must know that in each of these phases of the journey, *there's a high ground* for us, a better spot to place our feet, a place of refuge and protection. It's the place of nourishment, strength, and fruitfulness. It's the place of kingdom influence. It's in the center of God's will.

Though God offers provision for our missteps and Jesus is ready to meet us there when we fall or fail, there's a better place for us to walk. We're made and equipped to hike the high ground, a most fruitful, sacred place, appointed for us in every season, in every leg of the journey.

Discerning Your Season

Walking out God's highest and best purposes for us requires an ear bent toward heaven, a heart set on following Him, and eyes that see past the immediate circumstances. Obedience looks different in every season. Certain times call us to run when we'd rather rest, or to stand and fight when we'd rather run and hide.

If we want to lay hold of the life God promised us, we simply cannot take our cues from our emotional reactions to life circumstances (like I did last night). We lose ground every time we allow our emotional whims or selfish desires to win the day.

I've spent years pondering the whole idea of God's individual call on our lives and the specific and intentional ways He prepares His people for His purposes. I've noticed four specific seasons many believers walk through to lay hold of the powerful, uncommon life God offers us. I'll list all four below and then cover the first two seasons in this chapter, and the third and fourth seasons in the next two chapters.

What I've noticed is this: In every season, there's a high ground and a potential for forward movement. Sometimes we gain ground simply by holding our ground. Even so, we need not be at the mercy of the elements when the storms rage, and we must not lose perspective when it seems our life has come to a screeching halt. God can propel things forward in an instant when the time is right. We can trust Him.

These seasons teach us how to stand on what we know to be true in Scripture regardless of what we feel to be true in the present moment. We find great purpose in our steps when we know where to place our feet.

> God is my strong fortress, and he makes my way perfect. He makes me as surefooted as a deer, enabling me to stand on mountain heights. He trains my hands for battle; he strengthens my arm to draw a bronze bow.
>
> 2 Samuel 22:33–35 NLT

Four Seasons

Take a look at these four seasons and see if one stands out to you:

- ∿ Run—*Time to take ground* (times of favor and stretching faith)
- ∿ Rest—*Time to pull back* (times of refining and replenishment)
- ∿ Stand—*Time to hold on* (times of purifying and testing)
- ∿ Active Waiting—*Time to keep moving* (times of inward depth and forward movement)

We tend to move in and out of these seasons throughout our journey. In fact, sometimes we'll find ourselves in more than one season at a time as they may apply to different areas of our lives. It's important to discern your current season so you can better understand the enemy's strategy to derail you, and better discern God's plan to establish you. Let's start with the "run" season.

Run—Times of Favor and Stretching Faith

Years ago, I worked in the fitness industry and we often used this phrase: *Take more ground on the good days.* You know how every once in a while you wake up and just feel great? You're not sure what you did differently than other days, you just have more energy and clarity than you usually do. On those days we advised members to take extra ground in their physical fitness. We told them to run farther, lift more, push harder.

"Leverage this day to your advantage," we'd say. In one way or another, take more ground than you do on a typical day because a day is coming when you'll feel less than stellar and it'll be all you can do to show up for your workout. In order not to lose ground on those difficult days, you need to gain ground on the favorable days.

Let's apply this principle to life, especially a life in spiritual training. If you're in a season where the wind is at your back and things seem to come easier to you than they usually do, you might be in a season of favor, a time to run a very specific race marked out for you. Read the following passage:

> All athletes are disciplined in their training. They do it to win a prize that will fade away, but we do it for an eternal prize. So I run with purpose in every step. I am not just shadowboxing.
>
> 1 Corinthians 9:25–26 NLT

It's easy to settle into the mind-set that life is good because I am good. But in reality, life is good because God is good, and everything He does serves a greater purpose in our lives. This season of favor is a time to get focused, to make hay, to run with patient endurance. It's a time to do great things, to bear much fruit, and to make up for lost time. It's time to run with purpose in every step. This is not the time to sit on the couch of comfort and ease. And it's certainly not a time to dawdle with things that don't matter.

Sabbath rest and moments of replenishment are essential in every season of life, but I've found that in the "run" season, there'll be times when you want to rest and you even think you should rest, but God still calls you to run.

(A quick caveat: God calls us to regular Sabbath rest, which, if we fail to practice, we'll fall headlong into burnout. Even the "run" season involves regular Sabbath rest.)

I remember a particular season when I had quite a number of speaking events scheduled and I had a book to write. Lots of doors of opportunity opened up to me and quite honestly, I didn't really want to walk through them all. After experiencing burnout several years prior, I didn't completely trust myself not to go there again. So for years I erred on the safe side and said no more often than yes.

You can imagine my surprise in this new season when I brought these different opportunities before the Lord, asked for His direction, and more often than not He directed me forward, to take on more commitments than my personal inclinations would have allowed.

But each time I stepped forward in utter faith, He met me, strengthened me, showed up, and worked wonders through me. Just when I thought I had the whole personal boundary thing figured out, He blew it to smithereens. One way or another I had to learn to trust him more than my past experiences, and even more than my wisely gained logic.

In the midst of this intense season, Kevin and I had the opportunity to go to Guatemala with our friends from International Justice Mission. I had no idea how I'd survive an international trip on top of everything else, but we both knew God appointed us to take this trip. So we stepped up and stepped out.

Can you guess what happened? God parted the waters in our schedule. He provided the strength we needed. He opened doors for us to meet with government officials to talk about their efforts to protect children.

We witnessed firsthand the heroic work of IJM, and the Lord supplied ample content for my book. God changed our lives on that trip. Several people cautioned us about being too busy to take on such a trip. And realistically, they were right. But thankfully the logistics of our packed schedule didn't limit God's supply in any way.

During times of favor, we'll run, and then we'll run some more. We'll have more work than time to do it. This is the season where we see kingdom multiplication at work in us and around us. Opportunities will abound. God will call us to run farther than our flesh prefers, but it's in those stretching, growing places where we experience the Lord's divine efficiency and supply.

We'll never know or appreciate His unlimited supply until we exhaust our own. One important side note: Every opportunity is not a God-opportunity. And the need doesn't always dictate the call. We'll burn ourselves out if we try to seize every opportunity before us. It all goes back to staying in step and engaged with the Father, and doing only that which He gives us to do.

But even so, in this "run" season, we'll find ourselves doing more than even we think we should. It's a time of stretching, growing, and trusting God.

Temptations You May Encounter During the "Run" Season:

～ To dawdle, get distracted, and enjoy the wind at your back (totally missing the point of the season)

∽ To get tangled up in the affairs of this world

∽ To involve yourself in either time-wasters or good (but not God's *best*) time commitments

∽ To grow prideful because things are going well for you

∽ To loosen your grip on the Almighty because you're not aware of your desperate need for Him

If you don't run your appointed race during this time of favor, you won't feel the desperate need for God during this time. You'll miss out on the loaves-and-fishes miracles God typically provides during this season. On the other hand, if you do run in times of favor, you'll feel desperate for God and in awe of His faithfulness, all at the same time. Give what you have and God will do what He does.

Your High Ground During the "Run" Season:

∽ Do not neglect your private prayer times. *Make a daily appointment with Jesus and keep it.*

∽ Make yourself available to God. *Make your plan but let the Lord determine your steps* (see Proverbs 16:9).

∽ Keep your ear tuned to His voice; don't assume anything. *Stay engaged; refuse to be an autopilot Christian.*

∽ Open your hands regularly and receive His divine supply. *Daily He supplies. Walk forward in faith, counting on His faithfulness.*

∽ Remember, God multiplies what *He* assigns. *Do only what He gives you to do!*

∽ Rest when He tells you to rest and run when He tells you to run. *Trust Him. He knows what's up ahead for you.*

∽ Be okay with not understanding this season. It's a crazy time. *Trust in the Lord with all your heart and lean not on your own understanding* (Proverbs 3:5 NLT).

Scriptural Support:

And God is able to make all grace abound toward you, that you, always having all sufficiency in all things, may have an abundance for every good work.

2 Corinthians 9:8 NKJV

Rest—Times of Refining and Replenishment

The "rest" season is not typically a welcomed season for most of us. When God seemingly sets us aside for a period of time, it feels more like He's decided not to use us. We may view this season as a dismissal instead of a divine appointment. Though it feels otherwise, this season is an important part of a forward-moving process in our lives. And it rarely starts out feeling like a welcomed rest.

Maybe the season is better defined as "overlooked" or "out to pasture" or "God lost my address" or "Uh, hello? I thought we had a good thing going." More often than not, we either land in this season kicking and screaming or we find ourselves dead on arrival.

But either way, the intended outcome here is that we learn to rest in the Lord, learn to trust in His timing, give Him access to our character, and we come out the other side renewed, leaning on the arm of our Beloved.

This is the season where:

- ～ God reveals your motivations. *You discern how damaging your selfish ambitions can be.*
- ～ God heals your wounds. *You may hide in your busyness— but you need to slow down to heal.*
- ～ God restores your perspective. *You're reminded that Jesus is the Source, not your desires.*

- ∾ God refines your dreams. *You learn that God's dream for you is more significant than your momentary desires.*
- ∾ God strengthens your identity in Christ. *You understand—on a deeper level—how much God loves you and how little you can accomplish apart from Him.*

I stumbled into my season of rest years ago after a major burnout. My out-of-control schedule had taken me captive. Chafed and bruised, I curled up in a ball—my soul bone dry, my spirit withered, and my dreams wilted. I prayed for living waters to pour over me.

Disillusioned and appalled by my own ability to run myself ragged, I wondered how God could entrust a work to me when I so completely mistrusted myself. So many questions needed answers, so many unanswered prayers needed revisiting.

But once I stopped running and learned how to rest, moisture returned to my soul and a twinkle to my eye. Jesus loved me back to life, one cool summer breeze at a time. During those months of healing and recovery, my dreams took shape again, my energy returned. I stopped doing and just learned how to be. I learned to see the difference between a self-made ambition and a God-appointed desire. I found myself stunned by all of the ways God continued to work in me and around me without my help. Imagine that.

I prayed I'd never again try to serve God by pleasing man. Serving man leads us away from God. Serving God leads us toward loving and serving others, all the while keeping our hope in God and doing only what *He* says (not what others think we should do).

Though this season for me started out marked by pain and disillusionment, it left me forever changed. I learned that my Redeemer lives and that I will surely stand with Him on that last day. All else is rubbish compared to the surpassing greatness of truly knowing my Lord. I'm still gleaning from those months of hidden restlessness and rest.

Who is this coming up from the wilderness, leaning on the one she loves?

Song of Solomon 8:5 HCSB

Temptations You May Encounter During the "Rest" Season:

~ To run ahead of God and make something happen

~ To think you know better than God what is best for you

~ To think God has looked away or lost interest

~ To get restless when God is teaching you to rest

~ To get offended by and impatient with God for His "apparent" misunderstanding of the times

~ To despair over what seems like a dead end with no way out

~ To view this as wasted time or yourself as useless

Most of the time, the rest season starts painfully, but if we lean in and find the high ground of rest in the shadow of His presence, we'll find this to be one of the most sacred, grounding, purposeful seasons of our lives. Corrie ten Boom used to say "Don't wrestle, just nestle." Exactly. We make ourselves miserable if we fight when we're supposed to rest. We heal when we leave all of our cares in His hands and let Him put us right again.

Your High Ground During the "Rest" Season:

~ Delight in the Lord. *Learn to seek Him just for the sake of knowing Him more. More than the gift from His hand, seek to know His heart and the things He cares about.*

~ Lay down your agenda. *Put everything on the table, and let God speak to you about your life.*

⌒ See this season as God's protection over you. *Understand that when He makes you wait, it's because He's making you ready.*

⌒ Be humble and teachable. *Give God access to your ambitions, fears, and character inconsistencies; He'll transform and renew you.*

⌒ Cultivate a new level of intimacy with God. *Draw near to Him and He'll draw near to you.*

⌒ Start writing. *Once you stop wrestling and learn to rest, He'll put a new song in your heart. Write down what He shows you that others may benefit from your season of rest.*

Scriptural Support:

Since ancient times no one has heard, no ear has perceived, no eye has seen any God besides you, who acts on behalf of those who wait for him.

Isaiah 64:4

Still Waters and Sacred Spaces

Whether God has us in the land of opportunity with more tasks than time, or tucked away in a place of obscurity with little to do and where no one can find us, we must remember this: We're never out of His care, never far away from His heart. In every season, if we trust Him, He'll lead us beside still waters and to sacred spaces of replenishment and growth.

It's never His will that we run ourselves ragged. But He's more than okay with letting us endure a little fatigue when it comes to our stretching and growing.

And though He's after a return on His investment in us and cherishes the idea of forward-moving faith, He's also quite content to put us in seasons where there appears to be no forward movement, where life comes to a screeching halt. It's here where we learn that we're *not* what we do; we're simply someone He enjoys.

If you're in the "run" season, then run, my friend. With Jesus' heart beating in your chest, take on the giants, climb the mountains, and walk through the doors of opportunities before you. But never for a moment think that you can accomplish great things apart from God. And yet, live expectantly knowing that *nothing* is impossible *with* Him.

If you're in the "rest" season feeling broken and disillusioned, wrap yourself up in the comfort of God's love and faithfulness to you. He promises to make something new of you. He'll breathe fresh life into your weary soul. And He'll help you separate your self-sins from your divine purpose. Don't worry about forward movement in this place. Learn the essentials of rest and trust in this season, and one day you'll step into the best of what God has for you.

The "rest" season changed my life. Even though I still have moments of stress and worry, I can get back to that place of rest and trust far sooner than I ever could before.

After experiencing such a profound season of pruning and cutting back, I learned the critical lesson that life is found *only* in Him (not in the great things we do for Him). Now I see God's call for me to wait on Him as an *invitation* to enjoy deeper intimacy with Him. I no longer consider waiting a frustrating delay of my desires, but rather a call to purify my delight in Him. He's my greatest gift, my safest place.

The "rest" season also transformed my hubby's life. Even though Kevin still tends toward overcommitment on occasion, he is a kingdom man, through and through. Though the demands on his time and schedule are great, he humbly asks God for direction and balance every single day. And though he steps out of rhythm from time to time, he gets back in step quicker than he ever has before. We're both works in progress.

Just this morning I woke up overwhelmed by the piles of work before me: the hundreds of emails in my inbox, the stacks of sympathy cards waiting for thank-yous, the piles of laundry in the baskets, and the thousands of words I still need to write. My emotions of grief, gratitude, faith, and fatigue welled up within me at different moments throughout the morning and I couldn't seem to sort through them on my own.

And how did my husband respond to this struggling girl? He sat down and prayed with me. Then, still holding my hand, he walked me up to our bedroom, helped me create a sacred space to work, and then told me to get writing.

I held his face in my hands and kissed him first on the forehead and then on the lips. We're learning. We're growing. The high ground is such a beautiful place.

It's a moment-by-moment walk of faith and grace. We follow the Shepherd one sanctified step at a time. He leads us to high places and transforms us as we go.

Precious Lord,

Thank You for Your unrelenting, overwhelming love for and commitment to me. I open my arms wide, throw my head back, and ask You to pour that oil of anointing on my head. Pour out Your Holy Spirit afresh on me! Fill me up to overflowing so that I can live in the overflow of all that You are. Give me faith to run when You say run, and humble trust to rest when You say rest. Heaven will be perfect. And life down here is hard. But as I wait for that coming day, I want You to find me faithful, bearing fruit, and finding the high ground in every season of life. Lead me by still waters; lead me to those sacred spaces where Your presence is most tangible to me. I love You, Lord. Amen.

∼ STUDY QUESTIONS ∽

1. Read Mark 6:30–34 and write down which season (run or rest) this story best describes and why.

2. Read the section in this chapter on the "run" season again and read through the passage in Mark once more. What would have happened if the disciples had employed personal boundaries and decided they were done serving people for the day?

   a. Can you see how important it is to follow God's lead, even when we're weary? Write down your thoughts.

3. Read Mark 1:35. On one hand, we need to be available for God's divine interruptions in our day. On the other hand, we'll burn out without regular times with the Father. Describe a healthy balance between a disciplined devotional life and a flexible life of service.

4. Read Genesis 39:1–21 and notice how one minute Joseph prospered in the work of his hands, and the next he was falsely accused and thrown into prison (yet even there, God blessed him). The "rest" season is sometimes like the pruning process. Sometimes we're moving forward fruitfully and then suddenly set aside for a season because of the actions of another. What can we learn from Joseph's response?

5. In your heart, do you really believe God knows best when it comes to your different seasons of life? Why or why not?

6. Read Psalm 103:1–5 and write down a need you have for every promise offered (forgiveness for:____, healing for:_____, etc.).

7. Read the remainder of Psalm 103 and consider the contrast between our frailty and God's sturdy strength. Explain why it's important—in every season—to be found in Him.

∼⌒ DISCUSSION STARTERS ⌒∼

1. Can you think of a time when you wanted to rest and God called you to run? What happened?

2. As far as you can tell, what season are you currently in (run, rest, stand, active waiting)? Can you share a bit more?

3. Describe how a disciplined devotional life translates into a flexible life available and open to God's divine interruptions. Give some examples. (Also describe what happens when these disciplines become more about religion than relationship.)

4. Have you ever been (or know someone who's been) in the "rest" season? Can you share what you learned there (or observed)?

5. In your current struggle, can you identify the high ground, the most sacred space? What does life look like from there? How is He calling you to live differently than those around you?

Stay
the Course

You're blessed when you stay on course, walking steadily on the road revealed by God. You're blessed when you follow his directions, doing your best to find him. That's right—you don't go off on your own; you walk straight along the road he set.

Psalm 119:1–2 THE MESSAGE

No calamity will ever bring only evil to us, if we will immediately take it in fervent prayer to God. Even as we take shelter beneath a tree during a downpour of rain, we may unexpectedly find fruit on its branches. And when we flee to God, taking refuge beneath the shadow of His wing, we will always find more in Him than we have ever before seen or known.[1]

—Nathaniel William Taylor

Twelve years. He enjoyed twelve precious years with his little girl. He loved the way she skipped and played without a care in the world. He laughed when she'd giggle at the most nonsensical things. He couldn't fathom losing her now. He watched her tiny chest barely rise and fall with each shallow breath; she seemed to be slipping away before his eyes. Some religious ruler he turned out to be. He couldn't even save his own daughter. He'd do anything not to lose this little one he loved so much. *Dear God, intervene on behalf of my little girl!*

Twelve years. For twelve painful years, this woman trudged through life broken, exhausted, exiled, and alone. Ostracized from her community, they considered her unclean for reasons out of her control. Would her broken heart ever mend? Her body ever stop its hemorrhaging? Day and night, weeks and months all blurred together into one seamless struggle to exist amidst her failing health, with no one to comfort her.

She wiped the dust from her face and wondered, *What would it be like not to feel this frail? How would it feel to live in community again?* She struggled at the hands of doctors who guessed their best but found no cure. She spent the little money she had to get well, but to no avail. No one could stop the never-ending flow of blood from her body. Dirty, foul smelling, and at a loss for what to do, her condition made her an outcast. Dare she dream that a better life might be within her grasp? She blinked back her tears and prayed, *Dear God, are You up there? Do You care?*[2]

Read the following passage from the gospel of Mark:

> When Jesus had again crossed over by boat to the other side of the lake, a large crowd gathered around him while he was by the lake. Then one of the synagogue leaders, named Jairus, came, and when he saw Jesus, he fell at his feet. He pleaded earnestly with him, "My little daughter is dying. Please come and put your hands on her so that she will be healed and live." So Jesus went with him.
>
> 5:21–24

Jairus, a religious leader, publicly humbled himself (a big deal because Jesus wasn't too popular with Jairus's colleagues) and appealed to Jesus for help. Jesus responded and went with him. But something happened along the way. A certain delay brought great blessing and deliverance to one desperate woman but a devastating blow to an anxious father. Read on:

> When she heard about Jesus, she came up behind him in the crowd and touched his cloak, because she thought, "If I just touch his clothes, I will be healed." Immediately her bleeding stopped and she felt in her body that she was freed from her suffering.
>
> Mark 5:27–29

Immediately. Her bleeding stopped. *Instantly freed.*

Imagine that split second when sickness and weakness left her body: A rush of energized blood pulsated through her veins. Her cheeks flushed, her heart pumped hard, and her atrophied muscles rejuvenated, ready to be engaged.

In a moment's time, God restored this woman back to life. I'll bet she skipped through town. Scratch that. I'm thinking she sprinted through town and challenged sideliners to a race.

When God miraculously healed my son from a serious back injury after six months of pain, heartache, and minimal movement, he took off running, sprinted through the church parking lot, overjoyed to have his life back. I rejoice with this precious woman every time I read her story.

But wait. Imagine Jairus at this point. The sun coursed the sky; dusk came. His daughter faced death. Might be already dead. And while it was nice of Jesus to stop and help this woman in need, I'm sure Jairus would've rather seen his own daughter healed. I wonder if he struggled to compare their stations in life: he, a respected leader, and she, a ragged woman, an outcast, even. Don't you just love that Jesus made time to heal her?

Still, if I were Jairus, I'd have felt antsy and agitated. Let's read on:

While Jesus was still speaking, some people came from the house of Jairus, the synagogue leader. "Your daughter is dead," they said. "Why bother the teacher anymore?"

Mark 5:35

Talk about a fist to the gut. Can you imagine receiving such news? What kinds of thoughts ran through Jairus's mind? *Wait a minute. I asked first! Why did I even come here? Why did I make a fool of myself in front of my friends? Why did Jesus choose to heal this outcast over my precious little girl? Why, why, why?*

Just then, Jesus interrupted his thoughts with these startling words:

Jesus told him, "Don't be afraid; just believe."

Mark 5:36

In so many words Jesus said to Jairus, "Look at Me. Don't listen to them." Whatever thoughts ran through Jairus's mind in the heat of the moment, he decided to look up and trust in Jesus when it mattered most. Jairus accompanied Jesus and got his miracle.

Two unlikely people, while walking through their own personal storms, reached out to Jesus that day in a humble yet bold way: an outcast and a religious ruler. Both looked to Jesus and both found Him to be their solid Rock of refuge and received a life-transforming miracle from Him.

The Secret to Staying the Course

In the previous chapter we explored two of the four refining seasons we often walk through during times of preparation. Before we get into the third of the four seasons, let's examine two virtues that will help us stay the course when storms threaten to sweep over us. These two virtues help keep us on track and position us to receive the best of what God wants to give us, especially amidst the trials and challenges we'll face along the way: *humility and boldness.*

Jairus and the unknown woman with the issue of blood both possessed a certain tenacity mixed with humility. Scripture calls us to both humble ourselves under the hand of the Most High God (see 1 Peter 5:6) and to come boldly before the throne of grace in our time of need (see Hebrews 4:16).

Some come boldly before God but lack true humility. The result? A misplaced sense of entitlement. God owes us nothing. Yet He offers us everything through His Son Jesus Christ. Still, we have no business coming before Him with pounding fists and demanding hearts. The Pharisees tried this approach and, as you may have already noticed in the Gospels, it didn't go well for them. We can come before Him in this manner, but we won't get very far with Him either.

He's too good a Father to spoil His children or to give in to our misguided whims. Besides, it's rarely good for us to get what we want when we want it. Any sense of entitlement on our part proves a gross misunderstanding of who God is. Remember what Scripture says: "God opposes the proud but shows favor to the humble" (James 4:6). Jesus loves the humble heart. He can't get enough of it. He draws near, showers with grace, dwells within the humble, trusting heart. Why? Because it's a reflection of His heart in us. If the Savior of the world is supremely humble, how dare we be anything but the same?

Others dare *not* come boldly before the Lord because they struggle so with a constant sense of self-awareness. They come before God with a worm-like mentality that reveals a misunderstanding of their new identity in Christ. They're so focused on their lack, they totally miss God's promise of supply. Because of His victory on the cross, we've been made heirs of God and joint heirs with Christ (see Romans 8:16–18). Truly mind-boggling when you think about it.

Let's look at a few examples from the Word of God of how *humble boldness* moved the heart of God. The combination of these two attitudes is essential to mountain-moving faith and for standing strong while we wait for our breakthrough.

- From Matthew 8:5–13: A Roman soldier approached Jesus with a desperate need. His servant lay sick in bed, wracked with pain. This centurion appealed to Jesus to go to his home and touch the boy. Here we see the soldier embrace *humility*. He—as a man of recognized status—recognized Jesus as a man of even greater status and said to Him, "I'm not worthy to have you in my home . . ."

  But the officer was also *bold*. He continued (my paraphrase), "I understand authority because I have authority and am under authority. You can speak into my situation right here, right now, Jesus, and I know Your words will change everything." Jesus recognized this man's humility mixed with boldness as great faith, and his servant was healed that very hour. The only people on the planet that amazed Jesus were those with great faith and those with no faith. This centurion's faith inspired Jesus.

- From Matthew 15:21–28: A Canaanite woman desperately longed for her little girl's deliverance. A Gentile woman approaching a Jewish man? A *bold* move, indeed. Yet Jesus ignored her initial request. My guess is He wanted to teach His disciples a lesson about tenacity in faith.

  John Eldredge suggests we should picture a bantering twinkle in our Savior's eye as we read this story. This tenacious mother would not relent; she pressed Him again, asked for a miracle. This time Jesus answered her by explaining His mission.

  She petitioned Him again. Jesus answered with a harsh answer, "It isn't right to take food from children and throw it to the dogs." She came right back with a brilliant (*humble yet bold*) answer: "That's true, but even dogs are allowed to eat the scraps that fall from the table." In so many words she's saying, "I'm not appealing to you because *I* am good; I'm hanging on to faith because I know that *You* are good." Jesus responded with great affection, admiration, and an answer to her prayers: "Dear woman, your faith is great and your request is granted." Humility and boldness. A powerful combination.

From Luke 8:40–47: We explored this story at the beginning of the chapter. This poor woman suffered in unimaginable ways. She had the inferior stigma of being a woman and the negative stigma of her issue of blood (which, like leprosy, forced her to isolate from people; considered unclean). She lived with the horrible body odor caused from bleeding, the wretched and chronic fatigue, the loneliness of isolation, and the pain of living a just-get-by kind of life.

This woman lived as an outcast, separate from the people—until she couldn't stand it another moment. This exhausted yet brave woman broke tradition, pressed through the crowds, and grabbed a fistful of Jesus' garment. Her body healed instantly.

At that moment, Jesus turned around and asked who touched Him, because He felt healing power go through Him. She did not run away in fear. But how tempting it would have been in an attempt to hang on to her healing! She *humbly* bowed before Jesus and admitted that she was the one who touched Him. So brave, *bold,* and humble. I believe Jesus engaged her in this way so He could convey, "My precious soul, you didn't *take* healing from Me. I gladly gave it to you. Be healed and restored!" Can you imagine how she lived her life from that day forward?

Need a Fresh Revelation?

Do you need a fresh revelation of God's power and love? Have you lost sight of His glory, His awe-inspiring wonder? Do your problems appear bigger to you than your God? Do the mountains that stand in your way seem more immovable than God's love for you? Have you forgotten that He spoke the stars into place and told the water where to stop and the land to begin?

If so, maybe it's time to seek His forgiveness for losing sight of His greatness. Maybe it's time to open your arms wide and ask for a fresh revelation of God's love for you. The moment you pray such a prayer, you'll be wrapped up in His joyful love and His glorious acceptance, and in due time you'll find a renewed perspective of your place in Him.

Maybe humility is almost instinctive for you, but tenacity—well, not so much. How many times have you dared to ask God for the impossible? How often do you plant seeds of faith only to let those desires be choked out with weeds of worry and distraction? If Jesus walked in the flesh with you today, would He pause and marvel at your tenacious faith? Or would He be taken aback by your unbelief?

Do you need a fresh revelation of God's goodness? Has it been a while since you've reveled in the idea that He *loves* to do the miraculous in and through you? Small prayers and false humility do not bless or impress God. If you need a fresh measure of faith for the great things God wants to do in and through you, ask for it. Jesus loves audacious requests for more faith.

In his excellent book *The Circle Maker,* Mark Batterson tells about a friend who owned a log cabin on Lake Anna in central Virginia. Mark and his family vacationed there on occasion. During their first stay at the cabin, Mark decided to go for a training swim in the lake. Way in the distance he saw the oddest thing: a tree growing out of the middle of the lake. Curious, he decided to swim out and take a look. He came upon a tiny island about five feet in diameter, which boasted a single tree. As Mark got closer to the tree, he felt the ground beneath his feet. He literally stopped swimming and stood upright on the little island, smack dab in the middle of the lake.

Mark's family followed him in a boat and were quite a distance away when they saw him stand up. From their perspective, it looked like he walked on water. Mark wrote:

> That moment is more than a fun family memory; it's the mental image that comes to mind every time I think about standing on the promises of God. The promises of God are like that tree-island in the middle of the lake. They are the difference between sinking and swimming because they give you a place to stand . . . And when God keeps His promises, you won't just stand on the water; you will waltz into the Promised Land through waters God has parted.[3]

Standing Our Ground, Trusting His Promises

Last chapter we explored the first of the two seasons of preparation:

- Run—*Time to take ground* (times of favor and stretching faith)
- Rest—*Time to pull back* (times of refining and replenishment)

Now we'll take a look at the third season:

- Stand—*Time to hold on* (times of purifying and testing)

In the next chapter we'll explore the fourth season:

- Active Waiting—*Time to keep moving* (times of inward depth and forward movement)

Stand—Times of Purifying and Testing

Years ago when my kids were eating breakfast one morning, I found myself more under my circumstances than on top of them. During the worst part of my battle with Lyme disease, my fatigue, facial numbing, memory loss, and overall weakness felt like it might win the day. My boys all sat around the breakfast table, one in a high chair, one on a booster chair, and one on a couple of phone books. They were ready to party and I felt like I might pass out. I looked over my shoulder at the couch in the living room. Though only about ten feet away, it seemed easier to just lie down on the floor while my boys ate their breakfast.

Curled up in a ball, I took in some deep breaths and took in the sights from under the table. Hmm. *How and when did they manage to draw crayon pictures on the bottom side of the table? And who gave them gum? How long did they chew it before they stuck it under the table? I'm nothing like the mom I thought I would be, hoped I would be.*

Just then the boys busted out in song and giggles. With sweeping arm movements they sang their song and waved their spoons in the air. In one brief moment, one of them knocked their cereal bowl off the table and the soggy cornflakes and milk splattered over me on the floor. The boys giggled at first until they saw their momma sobbing. I couldn't help it. The mess on me reflected the mess in me. And I didn't have the energy to stand up and clean up. *Oh, Lord, where are You in this place?*

Strapped into his high chair, Jordan stretched out his sticky hands for his momma. He cried because I cried. He didn't like being stuck. Neither did I. Jake and Luke crawled down off their chairs, knelt beside me, and wrapped their arms around me. Soggy flakes and all. *It's okay, momma. Everything's going to be okay.* Though my soul groaned at the thought of being so low that my kids had to get on the floor to comfort *me,* the fact is I needed truth in that moment. And God spoke it to me out of the mouths of my children.

In the days that followed, I kept asking, kept seeking; *God, show me Your face and Your grace in this storm.* And eventually, He taught me how to stand up and stand strong amidst the turbulence around me. I learned to stand on His Word regardless of what my circumstances screamed at me.

In the morning I'd rise up out of bed, look in the mirror at my numb face to make sure it wasn't drooping (something I feared), and then I'd walk away from the mirror and look out the window at the endless sky. I'd put my hand on my face and say out loud, "I will not die but live and declare the works of the Lord (see Psalm 118:17). I will live out the number of my days in health. By His stripes, I am healed (see Isaiah 53:5). He forgives all of my sins, heals all of my diseases" (see Psalm 103:1–5).

I'd lift up my empty checkbook and declare, "My God shall supply all of my needs according to *His* riches in glory!" (see Philippians 4:19). I'd put my hand on my little towheaded boys and say, "You will be mighty in God someday" (see Psalm 112:2). I'd march around my house and say, "I will possess the land of promise God has for me. It *won't* always be this way" (see Psalm 37:10).

I have to say, along with King David, "It was good for me that I was afflicted." The following Psalm became my reality:

> My suffering was good for me, for it taught me to pay attention to your decrees. Your instructions are more valuable to me than millions in gold and silver. You made me; you created me. Now give me the sense to follow your commands. May all who fear you find in me a cause for joy, for I have put my hope in your word.
>
> 119:71–74 NLT

My "stand" season forced me to get off of the sinking sand of false security. Though I longed for temporary physical and material comfort, my trial compelled me to find shelter and firm footing on the Rock of my salvation. Do you know we're still reaping blessings today from standing in faith all those years ago? I'll share more about that in the next chapter.

If you're currently in the "stand" season, here's a great declarative promise on which to stand: "My victory and honor come from God alone. He is my refuge, a rock where no enemy can reach me" (Psalm 62:7 NLT).

The "stand" season is named as such because it seems the fury of hell is aimed at you, every storm at work to take you out. This is a tough season to endure. To gain ground in this season is simply to hold your ground, so as not to lose your ground. You have to grab hold of your inheritance promises and hang on for dear life.

During this trying season you may battle despair, disillusionment, and unbelief. You may feel the pull toward worldliness, entitlement, discontentment, and shallow faith. Don't let go of what you know to be true. And if you don't know who God intends to be to the storm-tossed soul, read His Word and find out, because it'll anchor your soul.

Temptations You May Encounter During the "Stand" Season:

- ∿ To look down and forget the promises of God
- ∿ To doubt much of what you know to be true
- ∿ To lose ground because you loosen your grip
- ∿ To look for shortcuts through the storm that takes you away from God's best will for you
- ∿ To develop a cynical attitude toward God when it comes to the suffering we (and others) endure on earth
- ∿ To listen to the voice of the enemy when God seems especially silent

If you're in a stormy season and feel completely under your circumstances, remember this: You stand upon the very Word of God, and His promises are backed by the honor of His name (see Psalm 138:2).

Staying the Course During the "Stand" Season:

- ∿ Remember in the darkness what He told you in the light. *Seek Him until you find Him. Find a promise for your problem, and with bulldog faith hang on to what God says is true.*

- ∿ Refuse lethargy, cynicism, and unbelief. *Do not let your faith-muscle atrophy. Engage your faith even when it hurts. Dare to trust God even when you don't feel like it. Guard your heart and mind against negative and unbelieving thoughts.*

- ∿ Don't let your heart close up here—stay tender to the things of God. *When you find your spirit closing up to the things of God, get with some godly friends, prayerfully ask God's forgiveness, and ask them to help you stay teachable and humble.*

- ∿ Deal with the issues that surface during this time. *No matter the reason for your storm, no matter if someone else is to blame, God will use this season to refine and purify you. Humble yourself and do the work of sorting through your stuff.*

- ∿ Know that in due time, the breakthrough will come. *Know this, say this, every day: "Any day now, I will see the deliverance of the Lord on my behalf. 'I will see the goodness of the Lord in the land of the living'"* (Psalm 27:13).

Scriptural Support:

Now therefore, stand and see this great thing which the Lord will do before your eyes.

1 Samuel 12:16 NKJV

Don't lose sight of the fact that God loves you, He's with you, and He has given you authority over your storm. Though the elements rage against you, they don't have the power to take you out. And always remember, the posture of humility before God (keeping a right perspective of Him) and boldness in prayer (keeping a right perspective of what you possess in Him regardless of how you feel or what your circumstances say) will help you not only stay the course but also become an unconquerable force. Read this powerful quote written in the 1800s by English clergyman George Body:

Thou are but His solider, guided by His wisdom, strengthened by His might, shielded by His love. Keep thy will united to the Will of God, and final defeat is impossible, for He is invincible.[4]

Precious Lord,

I know I'm not the only one feeling storm-tossed and perplexed by the challenges I'm facing right now. Though I may not be able to see or hear You, I know You are with me. Though the sky seems dark all around me, I know You are near. Nothing can separate me from Your love. No storm is stronger than Your grip on me. I will surely triumph in the work of Your hands. I humbly bow before You and worship You as my King. Have Your way in me and make me ready for my next place of promise. I boldly rise up in faith in this painful place, and I dare to ask you, Lord, put a dream in my heart! Show me what a liar that enemy is and reveal to me my next place of promise. I will possess the land by faith because You are faithful, Lord. Oh, how I love You. Amen.

STUDY QUESTIONS

1. Some think that God doesn't lead us into storms; He only delivers us out of them. Do you think that perhaps He allows the storms to show us the solidness of our Rock? Read Hebrews 12:26–27 and answer the following questions:

   a. What things in our world (and yours) are being shaken right now?

   b. Though it may be a difficult time, is this season revealing sturdiness in your faith?

   c. What of God's faithfulness are you learning now that you wouldn't have learned otherwise without the storm?

2. Read Hebrews 12:28–29. Now prayerfully, humbly read it again. Now let's apply it:

   a. Take a moment to write down the things in your life for which you are humbly grateful.

   b. Take a moment in your day to sit down, put your head back, play a worship song, and sing it back to the Lord for His great goodness to you.

   c. Open your hands, consider your God and God's promises, and then hold them close to your heart. If you've lost sight of God's majesty, now is a good time to humble yourself before Him.

   d. Write out a prayer expressing your love and appreciation for having access to the King of Kings and Lord of Lords.

3. Read Matthew 8:23–27 and notice how the disciples followed Jesus into the boat, which landed them right in a storm.

   a. Were the disciples out of God's will by getting into the boat with Jesus?

b. Yet Jesus corrected them. How did Jesus want the disciples to react to the storm?

c. How does He want you to react to your storm?

4. Read 1 Peter 4:12–13 and answer the following questions:

a. Even though Scripture tells us not to be surprised when hardship comes our way, do you still find yourself surprised? Why do you suppose that is?

b. To the extent that we suffer hardship as we follow Christ, will we relish our victories? Write about a victory you would have missed out on had you not gone through the storm battle.

5. Read Romans 12:12 and describe your current state as it relates to these three elements of this verse:

a. Joyful in hope:

b. Patient in affliction:

c. Faithful in prayer:

6. Read (and memorize) 1 Corinthians 16:13–14. Let this passage be an anchor to your soul.

7. Read 1 Corinthians 15:57–58 out loud (emphasizing words like: *give thanks, be steadfast, immovable, always abounding*). Now stand up, stomp your feet on the ground, and give thanks to God. Say loud enough for your own soul to hear, "I'm not moving from this place of faith! I will give what I have and the Lord will do what He does!" Let this verse be your defiant victory cry in the face of the enemy's threats and taunts. Give thanks. Be strong. Don't move from your faith stance. Soon, any day now, you will see the deliverance of the Lord.

⟶ DISCUSSION STARTERS ⟵

1. Warren Wiersbe describes two kinds of storms the believer experiences: "storms of correction and storms of perfection."[5] Scripture says God will not be mocked; what we sow is what we grow (see Galatians 6:7). Some of our storms are a direct result of our own poor choices. And while God can redeem our mistakes, He'll allow us to learn from the storm. Other times our storms are simply painful, refining, training times that prepare us for a purpose. Describe how both of these kinds of storms have played out in your own life.

2. What are the most common lies and defeating messages the enemy seems to use against women? What lies and defeating messages are you battling right now?

3. How do you stand against those lies?

4. What have you noticed strengthens your faith? What weakens it? (Are you able ask for help when you need it?) Why or why not?

5. Is there a verse or certain truth that God has been speaking to you about these days? What's He saying to you?

Take New Territory

So it's you who are in charge of keeping the entire commandment that I command you today so that you'll have the strength to invade and possess the land that you are crossing the river to make your own. Your obedience will give you a long life on the soil that God promised to give your ancestors and their children, a land flowing with milk and honey.

Deuteronomy 11:8–9 THE MESSAGE

Take
New Land

Take possession of the land and settle in it, for I have given you the land to possess.

Numbers 33:53

As we move forward in faith, simply and fully trusting Him, we may be tested. Sometimes we may have to wait and realize that "perseverance must finish its work" (James 1:4). But ultimately we will surely find "the stone rolled away" (Luke 24:2) and the Lord Himself waiting to bestow a double blessing on us for our time of testing.[1]

—A. B. Simpson

We wrap our fingers around the promises of God. We put one foot in front of the other and determine to keep walking, and eventually we'll most certainly possess the land God has for us. Our humble bold belief in God amidst each trial and refining season is *no small thing* to Him. He moves on every act prompted by our faith because our faith amid hard times is more precious to Him than gold. A little later in the chapter we'll cover the fourth season, the "active waiting" season. But first let's talk about taking new land, because by the time we arrive in the "active waiting" season, we'll have already taken some of the land God offered us.

Here are some of the landmarks from my own life—answers to earnest prayer, glorious moments when, after the storm and opposition, I stepped foot on to, and wiggled my toes in the green grass of promise God put in my heart to possess:

- When my kids (and other family members) received Christ
- The first time I rode fifty miles on my bike at a steady, fast pace (post-Lyme disease)
- The day we moved from a rental home into our own home
- Jordan's back miraculously healed
- Kevin's new job
- Waking up each morning to the sun peeking through the countless trees behind our backyard
- The huge corner we turned in our marriage after a long season of dryness, depletion, and miscommunication
- Ministering alongside my husband and going after audacious things in prayer with total agreement
- Watching my sons honor the women in their lives
- Going on my first international mission trip
- Signing my first book contract
- The day my middle son, Luke, married his godly wife, Kristen
- Watching them become a mighty kingdom couple
- Coming to a place of trust, transparency, and forward-moving faith with a few close girlfriends

- Going to Capitol Hill to lobby for legislation to help end the trafficking of children
- Giving ten times the amount we planned on to our church's building campaign
- Starting as a backup radio host, eventually getting my own show
- Seeing women miraculously transformed and restored before my very eyes at my speaking events

These are some of the places of promise God put in my heart, seeds of faith He put in my hand, when all I possessed at the time was a barren field of thickets and thorns. When circumstances spoke otherwise, God gave me faith to see my barren fields restored, to feel green grass under *my* feet (instead of just admiring it from a distance, in someone else's yard). He gave me eyes to envision the expanded territory that He lovingly assigned to me.

Then my great and wonderful Shepherd led me to my places of promise, one faithful step at a time. Read this powerful, personal verse: "The Lord directs the steps of the godly. He delights in every detail of their lives" (Psalm 37:23 NLT).

The other day a Women of Faith speaker, Angie Smith, joined me on my show. I asked if she had a Scripture passage that God's been speaking to her about these days. She shared the following verse: "He heals the brokenhearted and binds up their wounds. He determines the number of the stars and calls them each by name" (Psalm 147:3–4). She explained how on a family vacation cruise, her little girl met a woman battling cancer. Her young daughter scooted up next to the woman with no hair and began to share what she knew of God. "You see the sky? Jesus made it. You see the water? Jesus made that too. You see the birds? Jesus made them." Then she paused for a brief moment and said, "But I don't think Jesus can make a peanut butter and jelly sandwich."

This sweet story reveals her daughter's childlike heart, but Angie shared how it also reflects our own tendency to miss certain aspects of God's character. She reflected on how we believe His hand is big enough to set the stars in place, but not small enough to intervene in our lives in ways that really matter to us.

The wonderful, beautiful thing about God is that He is *as* capable of moving in our lives in intricate ways that everyone else might miss (but we notice), as He is of telling the water where to stop and the land where to begin. He's fiercely powerful yet lovingly gentle, effortlessly everywhere, yet intimately *right here.*

Whether you see it or not, you've definitely benefited from the smallness of God's hand in your life, the intimate, personal ways He's intervened in your circumstances, the gentle ways He's touched you, changed you, and ministered hope and healing to you. Since your name is written on God's hand, it's safe to say you're especially close to His heart.

Most likely right now you're standing on some of the land you prayed for (or that someone else prayed for you), or that God simply blessed you with because of His grace and goodness. Maybe it's your current job, a certain friendship, progress with one of your kids, a new season in your marriage, less stress in finances, a spiritual breakthrough with a neighbor, or the beginnings of a ministry dream come true. Today's a great day to give thanks for the countless ways God has cared for you with His strong yet gentle hand.

Do you want to know God's will for you in this place you now stand? Thank Him for what He's already done. The grass will turn green right under your toes! To *fully* possess your current territory, you need to remember how truly rich you currently are.

Do you want to get a glimpse of where He wants to take you? Pause first, and thank Him for how far He's brought you. Look over your shoulder for a moment, note your progress, and raise hands in thanksgiving.

Ingratitude and forgetfulness cause spiritual blindness and deafness. But when our mouths open in praise, our eyes look up too. That's when our next horizon comes into view. And when we look ahead through faith's lens, our ears more clearly hear the Shepherd's voice telling us, "I've been with you. I'll be with you. This is the way. *Follow Me.*"

Grace for the Journey

In the previous two chapters we covered three of the four seasons:

- ∾ Run—*Time to take ground* (times of favor and stretching faith)
- ∾ Rest—*Time to pull back* (times of refining and replenishment)
- ∾ Stand—*Time to hold on* (times of purifying and testing)

Now we'll explore the fourth season:

- ∾ Active Waiting—*Time to keep moving* (times of inward depth and forward movement)

As I mentioned in a previous chapter, it's quite possible to be in two of these seasons at one time, as they may apply to different areas of your life.

For instance, my niece Lisa is walking through both the "rest" and the "active waiting" seasons right now. She has a dream to be a stay-at-home wife and mother. Yet for four years, she worked in a high-stress job as the main provider while her husband went back to school to be a meteorologist.

She lived out of state, away from her family. Her husband's academic schedule left him unavailable to her as well. She worked in a job that required much from her but offered no joy or fulfillment. She endured long workdays and lonely nights. She'd be the first to say that she didn't always handle the struggle the way she'd hoped. Everything about that season of her life seemed to cross her will and quench her joy.

Yet amidst her daily battles, she prayed, she dreamed, she dared to believe that God had a next place of promise for her, one that matched the desires of her heart. But her daily grind tested her faith and her perspective. She struggled through her days, wanting so much to see God break through in her circumstances.

She longed for a life that involved time with her husband and children of her own. When her husband finished school, she was finally able to take a part-time, low-stress job. God brought her into a land of physical and emotional rest and restoration after the many months of carrying the weight of their financial responsibilities. This was a huge breakthrough for her.

And while she's grateful to be out from under the pressure of her old job, grateful to enjoy some sweet times with the Lord, grateful for the relief of the daily stress she once carried, she's brokenhearted over her battle with infertility. They tried for years to get pregnant, but to no avail. They even went through two heartbreaking failed adoptions.

In the meantime, they've become foster parents.

Watching my niece lay down her life day after day, month after month, for a little baby that's not her own, one that she'll have to return to a family once they get their lives together, absolutely breaks my heart and inspires me all at the same time.

Though it's not easy, Lisa sees the hand of God in her midst. She's seen too much of God's faithfulness to doubt Him. So she moves forward in faith and graciously stewards the responsibilities before her. She loves her little foster baby. Prays for him many times a day. Tells him how much God loves him. And at the same time she lifts up the deep longings of her heart, day and night, asking God to give her children to call her own.

While Lisa waits on God and entrusts her desires to Him, God is using her to change that little boy's life. My niece Lisa is a faith-hero and is most definitely in the active waiting season.

Her story is not over yet. She's asked God for a vision for her life, and with all her heart she believes her beautiful call involves raising children to love and serve the Lord. I pray with great expectancy as I watch her story unfold.

What is God saying to you about your next place of promise?

You know, He loves to speak to us about His divine desires for us. Imagine your child coming to you and saying, "Mommy, if I could live out your best dreams for me, what would they be?" Wouldn't you just sweep your child up in your lap and sing a song over her life? Well, it's the same with God.

We serve a star-breathing God whose promises are *for us* that we might live more boldly and faithfully for Him. He deserves our humble reverence. Jesus' victory on the cross gives us access to the throne to which He invites us to boldly come. Oh, the love of Jesus! Oh, the promises of God! Don't leave God's offer of a life redeemed and abundant to go un-apprehended. Don't let go of the wonder that He's made Himself available to *you*.

God knows that when He calls us, He's getting our imperfect selves. He knows we'll stumble and fall along the way, and He's made provision for our weakness. But in the high and low points of our journey, He wants us to engage our faith. Will we trust Him—whom our eyes cannot see, or will we lean more heavily on the sinking sand beneath our feet?

May we determine in our stormy seasons that nothing is *ever* impossible with God. May we rejoice that God loves to take the things that are "not," to nullify the things that "are" (see 1 Corinthians 1:27–28). Because we are *not* a lot of things.

The more we pray for vision, revelation, and faith, the more God fills us with desire and purpose. The more we lean in to Him during the painful refining times, the more He shows us what in us still needs to go before He takes us to a new land.

Since we are works in progress, may we hold tightly to these truths every step of the way: His promises are true. He means what He says. And He loves it when we live lives totally disproportionate to who we are.

By daring to dream with God, humbly trust His process, and live by faith, we'll develop an appetite for the impossible. Living in a way that constantly engages our faith will make us love God more today than all of our yesterdays combined.

Active Waiting—Times of Inward Depth and Forward Movement

Right now my husband and I are in the "run" season. We're managing far more today than we did during our season of burnout so many years ago. But this time it's different. Someone once said, "The devil drives but the Shepherd leads." *This time,* we're living in response to God's leading and not in reaction to our own striving. Everywhere we turn we see fruit, favor, and invitations to participate with God (and, as with every season, we face opposition, enemy attack, and discouragement on occasion).

But we're in the "active waiting" season too. You know you're in the "active waiting" season when you've already possessed a certain measure of land that God has promised you, and you're walking it out by faith, doing your best to steward the things He's entrusted to you.

But still, deep within your soul are certain unfilled desires that you can feel in your skin and in your bones. They're a part of you. From the outside you look like business as usual, busy, fruitful, and productive (and you are). But on the inside your heart deeply groans for and longs to see God break through in certain areas of your life. And you carry these desires with you everywhere you go. We're there right now in several areas of life. Let me explain.

As I mentioned earlier, several years ago we felt the nudge from God to, in the next ten years, get to the place where we're able to live on half of our income so we can give the other half away. We're on our way there, but we have a pile of college debt yet to pay off. We're pressing hard in prayer, gradually increasing our giving in faith, and trusting God to help us do this impossible thing.

My sons are wonderful guys, and we laugh our heads off when we're all together. Still, I see places in them that I know God wants to grab and transform. And my soul cries out to God as I wait. With all my heart, I believe they've only touched the edges of what God wants to do in and through them. Day and night, I am relentless in my prayers for them.

I have asthma and need daily medication for it. I can't eat any gluten, dairy, or soy, which takes a lot of fun out of food and makes travel not always easy. I deal off and on with insomnia. When I go too many nights in a row without sleep, my immunities weaken, making old symptoms flare. I have a constant loud ringing in my ears and I deal with TMJ. Every single morning I wake up and feel the pain and stiffness in my joints, the residual effect of Lyme disease. On the days I'm especially tired, my face goes a little numb—nothing like before, but still, I long to be symptom free, to be healed, to forget I ever had the disease. I so want to sleep soundly at night, to enjoy different kinds of foods with friends, to breathe easy, and to be able to run without pain. And so I pray.

We have the privilege of ministering to thousands of women each year, and we hear testimony after testimony of transformed lives as a result. And we're so grateful.

Still, I deeply hunger for many, many more women to be healed, strengthened, and mobilized. I want signs and wonders to follow us. I want every depressed woman to be *delivered on the spot*, every rejected woman to suddenly know she's *beautifully received*, every confused woman to step into *startling clarity* in a moment's time, every sick woman to *experience healing* right where she sits, and every single Christ-following woman to be *mobilized* to live out her call with bold, humble, and tenacious faith. I want more from God for the women I meet, and my soul groans and longs for a richer harvest.

I've got a wild and sometimes boundless imagination. So this verse gets me every time, but I'm constantly challenged to believe it:

> Now to him who is able to do immeasurably more than all we ask or imagine, according to his power that is at work within us, to him be glory in the church and in Christ Jesus throughout all generations, for ever and ever! Amen.
>
> Ephesians 3:20–21

How about you? What's on your list? Where do you want to see God move in your life? Do you dare to believe God for a life that goes beyond your own wild imagination? Can you imagine making an impact in this world that outlives you? Do you have a sense of where God is taking you? Are there deep soul desires in your heart that you can't let go of? Might you be in the "active waiting" season? God provides abundant grace to steward well your current blessings while you plant seeds for a future harvest. In Christ you have everything you need for life and godliness (see 2 Peter 1:2–3).

Temptations You May Encounter During the "Active Waiting" Season:

- ∽ To get distracted by your daily duties (and forget about the seeds you planted)
- ∽ To get so focused on your unfulfilled desire that you mismanage your current assignment
- ∽ To emotionally leave your current assignment before God physically moves you to the next place He has for you

- To get bitter over the delayed fulfillment of your desires
- To miss opportunities to forgive and remain pure in heart, which hinders your forward-moving progress
- To minimize your time in the Word and spend most of your time dreaming about your desires (this disconnects your desires from the Word of God, which morphs them into something you've conjured up on your own)
- To adopt a bored, tired-of-waiting, *non-expectant* mind-set

(My friend Mary DeMuth suggested I add the following four temptations to this list):

- To be so fretting about money that you can't see beyond it
- To believe (wrongly) that God doesn't want to bless you
- To blame others (or yourself) for your lack of forward momentum
- To overwork to the point of exhaustion, trying to accomplish God's dream in your strength (result: burnout)

It's far too easy to go on autopilot during this season, or to fall back in a rut of offense and unbelief, or to run ahead and strive on your own and *forget* all about the promises God wants to fulfill in your life. Determine to stay so close to the Father's heartbeat that you fully trust His provision and timing in every aspect of your life.

Talk to God about the desires of your heart, not in a begging, pleading sort of way (those kinds of prayers rarely leave us with more faith), but in a holy, confident sort of way. Pray from above your circumstances, not beneath them. For example:

Lord,

I trust You to take away any desires in me that are not from You, and to fulfill Your best plans and purposes for

*me. I know that as I delight in You, You'll establish me.
Give me a vision for my next place of promise. Help me
to be fully faithful right where I stand. I can do all things
when I do them with Your strength. Thank you for being
a God of Your Word. I believe that any day now I'll see
glimpses of Your glory in my life. I know I can trust You.
Thank you for being faithful.*

Care for and nurture the promise of God within you. Trust His timing for its fulfillment. Stay in community and be honest about your up-and-down emotions and perspectives. Sometimes you'll need friends to loan you their faith when yours wavers.

A word of caution here: Don't get so wrapped up in the unfulfilled desire of your heart that you stop tending to the garden God has already given you.

It takes great maturity to pull the weeds, remove the rocks, and cultivate an atmosphere for growth in a garden that no longer seems exciting or fresh to you. But if God has you there, the potential of life is there too. Look for His fresh mercies; ask Him about the seeds He wants you to plant there.

Make this a time of active waiting, of leaning in and listening. Bring the redundancy of your days before the Lord and ask Him to help you comprehend—on a whole new level—what is the exceedingly tremendous power at work in and around you because of Him (see Ephesians 1:18–20).

Opening your eyes to the work of His hands will quicken your heart to remember that you are on a pilgrimage. Though the days may blur together, your faith journey is most definitely leading you somewhere.

And the unfulfilled desires of your heart? Take those before the Lord, and *keep* them there. In other words, don't just leave those desires with Him, walk away, and forget about them. Definitely entrust your desires to the Lord and give Him full control. But continue to come before Him with thanksgiving, and remind your soul that He's actively engaged, working out the details of the things that matter most to you.

And know too that He's working in you, inspiring you to care deeply about the things that matter most to Him. As you press in to know His heart, *He'll* become more precious than the gifts of His hand.

Ask God specifically to show you this week that He sees you. That He's mindful of you. Ask Him to show up in a you-shaped way, a tender way, a way only you would discern as a love letter from Him.

Staying the Course During the "Active Waiting" Season:

∼ Spend consistent time with the Lord. *Spend time in the Word and give yourself time to listen for God's voice. Don't let feelings of boredom, unbelief, and discouragement take root; deal with them. Keep your faith fresh and expectant.*

∼ Remind yourself of His promises to you. *Learn to pray God's Word. Pray fervently even when you don't feel like it; speak His promises out loud so your own ears hear them.*

∼ Ask for strength and grace to be faithful in the "now." *The daily grind is where we greatly mature. Ask for mercy and grace; He'll give it to you. Look for Him in everyday ways; count the ways you see Him and offer thanks each day.*

∼ Allow God to refine your desires along the way. *Be humble enough to keep your desires on the table for God to rearrange and redefine; His version of your dream and life purpose is your best version.*

Scriptural Support:

You're blessed when you stay on course, walking steadily on the road revealed by God. You're blessed when you follow his directions, doing your best to find him.

Psalm 119:1 THE MESSAGE

But those who hope in the Lord will renew their strength. They will soar on wings like eagles; they will run and not grow weary, they will walk and not be faint.

Isaiah 40:31

What about you? Can you identify with the "active waiting" season? I suppose for every follower of Christ, we're always in this season to some degree, always living within the tension of daily God-given demands and deeply felt unfulfilled desires. A maturing journey indeed. Press in and press on. You have access to all the riches of heaven. It takes time for a significant, sudden moment to happen.

Keep praying.

Keep believing.

Keep walking.

Keeping reaching for God's best for you.

And at just the right time, according to God's glory and your readiness . . .

The clouds will break.

The waters will part.

And there'll be a way where there was no way.

That's who God is. That's what He does. He loves to do the miraculous through a humble, believing soul. Give Him the glory He deserves by giving Him access to your whole self. Wait till you see what He has in store for you.

Dear Lord,

Thank you for teaching me about the beauty of my need because it leads me to the riches of Your supply. I no longer need to fear my shortcomings because the truth is, I'm a beautiful work in progress, thanks to You. I humble myself before You. I open my hands, my mouth, and my ears and I ask You to fill them. Fill me up to overflowing with more of You, more of Your insight, wisdom, and revelation. Impart to me Your dreams for me. Give me faith and courage enough to lay hold of them. You are so mighty yet so intimate, so strong and yet so gentle with me in my process. How can I ever thank You enough? I will thank You with my life. This is my offering of praise. Help me to live in a manner worthy of You and everything You've made available to me. Amen.

⁓ STUDY QUESTIONS ⁓

1. We read in Numbers 13 how God told Moses to send out men to explore the Promised Land. Read Numbers 13:27–33 and write down the differences between Caleb's report and the rest of the men's report.

2. God sent these men out to show them the land He wanted to give them. If God orders it, He'll establish it! These men saw the potential of the promise, but the process seemed impossible to them. Read Numbers 14:1–10 and answer the following question: How did their unbelief impact their community?

3. Read Numbers 14:11–12 and describe God's response to their unbelief.

4. We don't often realize that to embrace unbelief and to be unwilling to take faith risks is to hold God in contempt. Read Numbers 14:22–23 and write down the cost of their unbelief and complaining attitude.

   a. In what ways has your life been impacted by your own unbelief?

5. We may stand together in a group, but we stand before God as one. He responds to individual faith. He loves it when two or more gather in His name, in full agreement

that He is God, and He is faithful. But if only one in the group believes, He'll respond to one. Read Numbers 14:24 and explain why God promised to bless Caleb.

6. Read Numbers 14:34 and ponder this thought: The Israelites (with the exception of Joshua and Caleb) missed out on the Promised Land. God assigned them to roam the wilderness for forty years for the forty days they surveyed the land, and they gulped down unbelief when God expected them to rise up in faith. Is God showing you a next place of promise? What seems more immovable to you right now? God's promises? Or the impossibility of it all?

7. Read Numbers 14:31 and restate what the Israelites predicted would happen to their children.

   a. God in His grace didn't fulfill their predictions, but Scripture does have a lot to say about the power of the tongue. Read Proverbs 18:21 and answer the following question: Do your own words (and predictions) bear witness against you, or are your words seasoned with faith and hope? How we speak about our trying circumstances reveals what we think about God in that moment.

⌒ DISCUSSION STARTERS ⌒

1. Can you think of a time God put a promise in your heart? Did you respond by telling Him it can't be done? Or did you move forward in faith? What did God teach you through this process?

2. Looking back over the past few years, what landmark ways have you seen God's amazing faithfulness?

3. Looking back over the past few months, in what ways have you seen God's up-close-and-personal touch in your life?

4. When you consider the "active waiting" season, what current territory has God called you to faithfully steward? What challenges are you facing along the way?

5. As you steward your current place of promise, what deep soul longings are you trusting God for? Will you share one or two of your heart's desires?

12

Last Long
Finish Strong

And I am certain that God, who began the good work within you, will continue his work until it is finally finished on the day when Christ Jesus returns.

Philippians 1:6 NLT

Within my soul I feel the evidence of my future life. I am like a forest that has been cut down more than once, yet the new growth has more life than ever. I am always rising toward the sky, with the sun shining down on my head. The earth provides abundant sap for me, but heaven lights my way to worlds unknown.[1]

—Victor Hugo

In 1916, Hetty Green—known as the world's greatest miser—died with an estimated worth of over one hundred million dollars. Yet she ate cold oatmeal in the morning because it cost money to heat her breakfast cereal. Her own son suffered a leg amputation because she took too much time searching for a free clinic when she could have paid for his immediate care. Hetty died of a stroke-like condition while arguing over the cost of skim milk.

William Randolph Hearst, the wealthy newspaper mogul who got his start in the late 1800s, invested a fortune collecting art treasures from around the world. One day he read a description of several valuable pieces he just had to own, so he sent his agent abroad looking for those rare pieces of art. After an expensive several months of searching overseas, Mr. Hearst's agent returned with some good news: He found the pieces. Mr. Hearst *already owned them*. They were in his warehouse and he didn't even know it.[2]

Hetty didn't know who she was. Randolph didn't realize what he possessed. Before we judge them too hastily, we have to be honest with ourselves. Scripture tells us that God has blessed us with *every* spiritual blessing in the heavenly realm. Do you live with a continually increasing awareness of all you possess in Christ? Are you *growing* in the knowledge of God and embracing on a deeper level what He has freely offered you? Or more often than not, do you live like a spiritual pauper? I know I've got a long way to go in this regard. I've only touched the edges of His promises. I've dipped my toe in a Dixie Cup while the ocean remains. Far too often I live beneath my privileges, far beneath God's promised provision for me. Like Hetty, I sometimes live like a pauper when Jesus died to make me an heir.

And what can we learn from William Randolph Hearst? Though he owned vast amounts of wealth, he didn't feel satisfied. Practically jealous of himself, his desire for the next thing made him miss the things he already owned. We do the same thing. When we look to the left and the right (at what others possess) and forget to look up (to better understand what we possess), we overlook just how enormously rich we really are.

Who we are and what we possess. These are the two targets the enemy aims for again and again. If he can get us to doubt, he can trip us up. If he can get us thinking we're poor though we're really rich, we'll scratch and claw our way through life; we'll live anxious and afraid, like we're without hope.

And if he can convince us we lack something good, he'll be able to tempt us to live frantic and hurried lives, never satisfied, always wanting more. We'll skim life's surface and miss its depths. We'll live jealous, me-focused lives and forsake the whole reason we're blessed: Because God loves to love us, and He loves to love through us. Jesus promises that those who trust Him *lack no good thing* (see Psalm 34:10).

These aging earthen vessels carry the treasure of heaven within. Ponder the significance of that truth every single day. Read these two powerful verses and let them soak in your soul for a few moments:

> All praise to God, the Father of our Lord Jesus Christ, who has blessed us with *every spiritual blessing* in the heavenly realms because we are united with Christ.
>
> Ephesians 1:3 NLT, emphasis mine

> We now have this light shining in our hearts, but we ourselves are like fragile clay jars containing this great treasure. This makes it clear that *our great power is from God, not from ourselves.*
>
> 2 Corinthians 4:7 NLT, emphasis mine

Every spiritual blessing. The power of God mightily at work within.

If we dare turn a deaf ear to the enemy and listen only to heaven's song over us, we will take new land. We'll walk with holy confidence and humble dependence. We will grow bold in our faith. We'll go places we could never otherwise go. We'll be transformed as we go. We'll partake in loaves-and-fishes miracles.

And at different times we may be tempted to think we're something apart from Him.

"Marvel Because You're Mine"

After a mind-boggling adventure of miracles and ministry, the disciples returned to Jesus and exclaimed: "Lord, even the demons submit to us in your name" (Luke 10:17). Imagine their excitement, participating in everyday miracles, seeing lives and communities transformed before their very eyes. Their spiritual authority in Christ exceeded any earthly authority in their midst. I can picture them running up to Jesus wide-eyed and breathless to tell Him all about the countless God-moments they had just experienced. I'm sure they expected Jesus to jump up and down with them.

Jesus' calm, wise response is as much for us as it was for them: "I saw Satan fall like lightning from heaven. I have given you authority to trample on snakes and scorpions and to overcome all the power of the enemy; nothing will harm you. However, do not rejoice that the spirits submit to you, but rejoice that your names are written in heaven" (Luke 10:18–20).

In so many words Jesus said to them and says to us:

Yes, as you walk with Me and learn from Me, you'll get to do some amazing things in your lifetime. Be grateful when you see breakthrough, when I use you. But keep your awe focused on Me. Don't marvel at the great things you get to do, marvel at the great thing I've already done. I won the victory. I saved you! Marvel instead that your name is written in the Book of Life! Never allow the wonder of the things I do through you to upstage the miracle I've done in you.

As you follow Me and trust Me, you'll find that you're never too small for big things and never too big for small things. Humbly, boldly serve Me in the high and low places of life. But marvel every day that I saved you, that your sin is blotted out completely, that every act prompted by your faith is written down for future reward. I've redeemed you in every sense of the word. You're no longer an orphan, you're an heir. Live from *that* reality.

Years ago I met a woman who constantly talked about how often she ministered to people. More often than not, she'd say things like, "Everywhere I turn, I'm praying for people and ministering to them," or "We've ministered to folks the last three out of four nights just this week." To be honest, at first I felt enamored by her influence and her heart for people and for Jesus, but eventually I noticed something that distracted me: *her*. Rarely did our conversations leave me thinking more about Jesus. Most of the time I only noticed her.

I'm sure she meant well. And I know she loved Jesus. But it makes me wonder how often my own thoughts and words point to what I do more than what Jesus has already done. Our deeds are like a rug: a place to go facedown that we may offer up our actions and ourselves to the living God. But if we try to stand on those deeds for any kind of merit or attention, that enemy of ours will pull the rug right out from under our feet. I don't know about you, but I'd rather willingly bow down in honor to God than get knocked down while honoring myself.

To last long and finish strong, we must remember and believe with all our hearts that we can possess and produce no good thing apart from God.

No Self-Importance in the Kingdom

In Genesis 11:4 we read that the people wanted to build what we know as the Tower of Babel: "Come, let's build a great city for ourselves with a tower that reaches into the sky. This will make *us* famous and keep *us* from being scattered all over the world" (NLT).

Let's make a name for ourselves. And let's protect our interests. This temptation is alive and well today. If we take God at

His word, follow His lead, trust His promises, and endure times of testing, we will see eventual breakthrough, we'll put our toes onto new territory. And it'll bless our socks off.

But we'll also run the risk of marveling at our own abilities, making it about us, taking the credit, and thinking we're something apart from God.

We're not necessarily called to be successful, but we're most definitely called to be constant, devoted, and true. But sometimes this kind of faithfulness leads to success, and when it does, we risk losing our way. How much of God's blessing can we handle before we make it all about us? How many good things can He entrust to us before we believe that life is good because we are good?

Have you ever noticed how some successful people turn territorial? They're threatened by the up-and-comers, they grow insecure around people more anointed and gifted than they are.

Just when did their focus shift from Christ and His kingdom to themselves and their territorial footing? I wonder how many moral failures could be avoided if we were more sensitive to the motivation behind our efforts.

Don't you especially love it, though, when God-appointed successful people remain humble and gracious and fully dependent on Christ year after year, in spite of their very real and continual success?

My friend Sara Groves is a great example of a woman who is in it for the long haul. She's one of the most unassuming people I know. And though her music reaches far and wide and many admire her, she wakes up every day with a heart reliant on God. She knows she needs Him. I love serving side by side with her. When I'm with her, I forget she's successful and I remember afresh that God is good and that He is faithful. Her life, her convictions, and even her humor make me think of Jesus. She knows in her core that she's not "what" she does. She's simply someone God greatly loves. Knowing Sara makes me love Jesus more. I pray I have that kind of impact on people.

Some of my most favorite guests to have on the radio show have been high-profile, humble, gracious people. They're grateful for the opportunity to share what God has shown them. They treat you like they have all the time in the world for you. They point constantly to Jesus. And they don't take themselves too seriously.

And a few of my least favorite encounters have been with mildly successful, self-important, prideful people. You feel like they're talking to you while looking over your shoulder for someone more interesting or important than you. You get the sense they've arrived and that you're lucky to breathe the same air they do. Encountering the stench of self-importance makes me want to run to my secret place of prayer and cry out, *"Lord, I want my whole life be a fragrant offering to You! I do not want to trust in myself or believe in myself. I want to trust in You, believe in You! Yet how can I know all the sins lurking in my heart? Cleanse me from these hidden faults! Keep back Your servant from presumptuous sins! Don't let them control me! Then I'll be free of guilt and innocent of great sin"* (see Psalm 19:11–13).

It's wise to allow our encounters with prideful people to serve as a cautionary tale to teach us a different way to live. We can be sad for them, we can pray for them, and we can humbly ask God to protect His likeness in us.

The Lure of Fame

We're called to faithfulness. And yet we naturally long for success. And that's not a bad thing. But God calls us to seek His kingdom, His way, on His terms and His timing. Can we humbly, graciously follow and obey not only when it costs us, but also even when it pays huge dividends? Our success tests our hearts every bit as much as our struggles, just in a different way.

Since God provides everything we need for life and godliness, may we *refuse* a petty, jealous, or even territorial mind-set. May we throw off any tendency to stand on our laurels. When we encounter bold breakthroughs and great success, may we drop to our knees, humbly offer praise and thanks to God, knowing every good gift comes from Him. With every success and victory, may we look up and marvel that He saved us.

Any striving we do out of insecurity or jealous ambition will be like soot in our hands when it's all said and done. Those efforts will burn and leave nothing but ashes behind.

And yet when we lovingly offer a cool cup of water to a dry and parched friend who because of her thirst has forgotten who she is, our sacred offering goes with us into eternity. Instead of hands smudged with soot, we'll have hands filled with fruit. Oh, to be motivated by love and to live by faith with every word, every step, and every gift.

There's more than enough work to go around. According to Jesus, the work still exceeds the workers. He asked us to pray for more laborers, not to be threatened by the few (see Matthew 9:37–38).

Read this powerful passage from 1 John:

> Practically everything that goes on in the world—wanting your own way, wanting everything for yourself, wanting to appear important—has nothing to do with the Father. It just isolates you from him. The world and all its wanting, wanting, wanting is on the way out—but whoever does what God wants is set for eternity.

> 2:16–17 THE MESSAGE

When we humbly embrace the reality of who we are in Christ Jesus, we actually become vessels heaven uses on earth, to move God's purposes forward.

The Tree of Life

The other day a woman posted this note on my Facebook page:

> I want you to know we were at a women's retreat and heard
> you speak last October in Green Lake, Wisconsin. One of the
> ladies that came with us accepted Christ as her personal Savior.
> Early this past Sunday morning, she passed away. She was only
> 46 years old. We know God worked out so many details for her
> to even come to that retreat. That was her time to meet Him.
> Thank you Susie for being led by and being faithful to God.
> We can truly rejoice knowing that we will meet her again. She
> had just told our pastor the week before she passed that God
> had opened the eyes of her heart back in October at the retreat.

After reading this note several times, I sat at my desk and cried
grateful tears. Oh, the love of Jesus. *All glory and honor to You,
Lord. Thank You for allowing me to participate in this miracle.*

Later that same day, I returned from lunch to find a package that had been sent to the radio station and addressed to
me. The sender wrote these words on the package: *Unwanted
Material.* I gulped a bit as I tore open the package. I found a
copy of one of my books and a nasty handwritten letter from
a woman who in the last several months has sent me a handful
of strange, accusatory emails.

Over the months I tried to reason with this woman and understand her perspective, to no avail. She had it in her heart to be
offended by me no matter what I had to say. She had apparently
received one of my books through the radio show but decided
she wasn't at all interested in reading it. She mentioned in her
handwritten letter that she had tried to call and apologize, but
that I wouldn't accept her apology (never happened) and thus
wrote, "I don't believe anything you say. I don't respect you.
May God deal with you!"

I put the letter down and shook my head. I had to go on the
air in just a few minutes, yet I felt like I'd just been slugged in

the gut. I asked God to bless and forgive this confused woman and to heal both of our hurts. We had a great show that afternoon, but deep inside, this woman's anger toward me tied me up in knots.

I got home from work, changed clothes, and took my dog, Memphis, out for a walk on the trails. Brisk exercise with my muscle-bound pup is one of my favorite pastimes. But this particular day I went through the motions without enjoying the moment. My mind wandered to this woman. I felt so frustrated that I couldn't get through to her, so bummed that someone detested me with such fierce determination.

Like a sled dog, Memphis pulled hard on his leash and pulled me along with him. Suddenly the Lord whispered across my heart: *Look up.* I looked up to see two lone trees in a field, side by side. The whisper came again: *There were two trees in the garden.* "Yes," I replied. "The Tree of the Knowledge of Good and Evil and the Tree of Life." The Lord whispered again: *Which tree do you want to eat from? Which fruit do you want to eat?* I spoke in a subtle whisper, "I want to eat from the Tree of Life."

Years ago I read a book by Rick Joyner titled *There Were Two Trees in the Garden.* I pulled it off the shelf after my walk that day. Read what he has to say about the Tree of the Knowledge of Good and Evil:

> The knowledge of good and evil kills us by distracting us from the One who is the source of life: The Tree of Life—Jesus. The Tree of the Knowledge causes us to focus our attention upon ourselves. Sin is empowered by the law; not just because evil is revealed but the good as well. It drives us either to corruption or self-righteousness, both of which lead to death.[3]

When I focus on the right or the wrong things in me, my focus is on flesh, which leads to death. But when I focus on the miraculous, redemptive work of Christ in me and around me, life happens. Scripture tells us that from the focus of our hearts will flow the issues of our lives (see Proverbs 4:23). When we *fix our eyes* and *set our hearts* on either the great or terrible things we've done, or the great or terrible things others do, we'll give birth to more of the same. Read this passage from John 3:6: "Flesh gives birth to flesh, but the Spirit gives birth to spirit."

Seek First His Kingdom, He's Got You

Part of what it means to eat from and be nourished by the Tree of Life is to shift our focus from our efforts, even as Christians, *to Christ,* who valiantly saved us. Instead of feeding on our strivings, we're nourished by and built up because of the finished work of Christ on the cross. The power of His resurrection is what transforms us from the inside out.

Read Galatians 2:20: "I have been crucified with Christ, and I no longer live, but Christ lives in me. The life I now live in the body, I live by faith in the Son of God, who loved me and gave himself for me." Here's another verse to ponder: "For it is we who are the circumcision, we who serve God by his Spirit, who boast in Christ Jesus, and who put no confidence in the flesh" (Philippians 3:3).

What does it mean then to seek first God's kingdom and His righteousness? It means that we do *His work* under the new identity and authority we possess *in Him.* We stay hidden in Him for our protection and provision.

When we bear much fruit (which we will), He gets the credit. When we encounter opposition and mean-spirited people (which we will), we entrust our souls to Him. He'll defend and deliver us. We need not fear man because we serve an all-powerful God. When He gets the credit for the fruit that comes from us, He also takes the responsibility for the arrows others shoot at us.

Since my focus shifted from this woman's heart toward me to God's heart toward me, I also discovered God's precious heart toward her. I find myself praying for her with great love and compassion. Her opinion has lost its power over me because

God's opinion of me (and of her) has won me over. Spirit gives birth to spirit.

Finish Strong!

If you are the woman who started this journey with a buried dream in your heart, I pray you now believe and know that God is at work in and through you! And He is training you for greatness. May you trust Him every step of the way.

And if you're the woman who has been beaten down by life, wearied from the sameness of it all, I pray you've experienced a fresh flutter of hope in your soul. And I trust God will take you by the hand and lead you to a vibrant place of promise. May He surprise you with His goodness.

And if you're the woman who didn't at all resonate with words like *dream* or *calling* when you first started this journey, I pray you do now. I pray God has given you a fresh perspective on your beautiful purpose. I pray you see new opportunities to engage your faith and deepen your influence. May you know—on a deeper level—how much God loves His design in you.

Whether yours is a call of hidden significance or public influence, we all want to last long and finish strong. We want to run the race marked out before us with focus, passion, and conviction. But we can't keep ourselves on track by hanging on to our bootstraps or by any self-improvement method. Only the life of Jesus in us allows us to defy the gravity of our self-sins.

Only Jesus can keep us from tripping over ourselves and doing a permanent face-plant in the dirt. We may stumble a bit here and there, but we're going to finish this race by the grace of God in Christ Jesus. *He* will keep us strong to the end as we trust in Him and guard our own hearts.

Here are four boundaries, or core values that have helped keep my priorities straight and keep a watch on my motives as I walk this narrow road. Perhaps they'll help you too:

- ~ Holy Confidence (not insecurity and not a bloated sense of self-importance; a total belief that we are completely valuable and secure in Him)
- ~ Humble Dependence (not false humility and not a spirit of independence; a knowledge that we can do nothing apart from Him; we need Him every hour)
- ~ Kingdom Passion (not selfish ambition and not a passive lethargy; we're fueled every day by the life of Christ Jesus mightily at work within us; His priorities are our priorities, His passions are our passions)
- ~ Calvary Love (not self-preservation and not self-promotion; we die daily that we might grow deeper; we choose humble, sacrificial love, knowing that our salvation and our honor depend on God alone)

As we guard our hearts, keep His Word close and alive inside and the enemy's lies at bay; the Lord Himself will strengthen and energize us to endure. And the enemy's schemes against us? They'll come to nothing. We *will* finish strong, my friend!

I absolutely cherish this promise:

> To him who is able to keep you from stumbling and to present you before his glorious presence without fault and with great joy—to the only God our Savior be glory, majesty, power and authority, through Jesus Christ our Lord, before all ages, now and forevermore! Amen.
>
> Jude 1:24–25

You have this one life to live. What will you do with what Christ has offered you? Will you waste your energy trying to present an exaggerated version of who you really are? Will you strive to save face and pretend you're not insecure? Remember, flesh gives birth to flesh.

Or will you get real, face down your fears, and embrace the God-confident, significant life you were made for? Will you live in the knowledge that you're deeply loved, powerfully called, and profoundly equipped to change your world? I challenge you to wake up every morning with these words on your lips: *Every day I'm in Your presence, Lord. All that You have is mine. I have more than enough to live abundantly today. May the power of Your life in me energize all I say and do. Anoint my every choice and every word so when others encounter me, they encounter You. I live by faith and I am alive to God! Amen.*

May God open your eyes to all He has imparted to you! I dare you to dream with God, listen for His voice, and walk out His plan for you. I promise you, you'll be so glad you did.

Let's live out the promises of God together and be a people who live ready, prepared, and focused for Christ's return. When He comes again, may He find us full of faith and living abundantly fruitful lives.

May we stay humbly dependent on Jesus, hold unswervingly to His promises, and finish this race full of passion and abounding in love. With all my heart, I believe it's not only our call—by His grace it's utterly possible.

I'll wrap up with a blessing for you:

May you believe that your wildest dreams can come true. May you trust Jesus enough to follow Him through the valley to lay hold of them. May you be patient and purposeful in every season. May your selfish ambition die and your holy ambition arise. Then you'll be poised to change the world. Overwhelming victory belongs to you because you belong to Jesus.

Dear friend, thank you so much for allowing me to do this journey with you. Continue on in faith. Know that I'm praying for you! God bless you, dear sister.

Precious Lord,

I'm ready to follow where You lead! I want to live out the beautiful purpose You ordained for me before I was even born. Help me remember that an un-appointed work is an unanointed work. Give me the passion to do only that which You've given me grace to accomplish. By faith I repent of and reject selfish ambition, envy, pride, insecurity, and self-absorption. Instead I embrace Holy Confidence and Humble Dependence, Kingdom Passion and Calvary Love. Fill me up to overflowing so that my life becomes a wellspring of life to everyone I meet. Pour out Your Spirit on me in increasing measures so I will last long and finish strong. I'm ready to do exceedingly above and beyond all that my mind can conceive, according to Your work in and through me. I'm all in, Lord. Lead me on and glorify Your name in me. Amen.

STUDY QUESTIONS

1. Read Mark 6:1–3 and answer this question: Why do you suppose some people get offended or bothered when we do something significant? (Give me more than the obvious word: *jealousy*. What's underneath it all?)

   a. When others get offended by God's blessing on our lives, we can either react to them or respond to God. Recall a time in your life when you were jealous and describe how you handled it. Do you have a different perspective on that experience now than you did when it first happened? Explain.

2. Read Matthew 25:14–18 and note the two motivations represented in the three men in this story (the two men intended on giving a return on the investment, the third

man was motivated by fear). Are you more motivated to see God's fruit multiplied in your life, or more motivated by self-preservation and fear? Explain.

3. Read this study note from my NIV Bible: "The parable of the talents warns us that our place and service in heaven will depend on the faithfulness of our lives and service here (v. 29). *A talent represents our abilities, time, resources, and opportunities to serve God while on earth. These things are considered by God as a trust that we are responsible to administrate in the wisest way possible.*"[4]

   a. On the left side of a sheet of paper, write down these words, one underneath the other: *Abilities, Time, Resources,* and *Opportunities to Serve God.* Next to each of these words, write down how you stewarded each of these in the last week.

   b. Write out a prayer asking God to increase your capacity to live for Him that He might multiply His work in you.

4. Read 1 Corinthians 3:12–15 and consider this: Some believers—when they get to the end of their lives—will have nothing to show for their lives lived on earth. They'll be saved, but their work on earth will burn to ashes. Any and everything we do out of our flesh (self-sins, self-preservation, self-promotion), will not survive the flames. But the simplest cup of water given out of love for Jesus will make a big splash in heaven. God celebrates every act prompted by our faith but disregards every act prompted by our flesh. As believers, we won't face the great white throne of judgment (reserved for unbelievers), but our work will go through the fire. Only what's done for Christ, by faith, will outlast us.

   a. Based on the seriousness of your call, and thinking from an eternal perspective, do you feel led to make any life adjustments?

5. Read *The Message* paraphrase of Galatians 6:4–5: "Make a careful exploration of who you are and the work you have been given, and then sink yourself into that. Don't be impressed with yourself. Don't compare yourself with others. Each of you must take responsibility for doing the creative best you can with your own life."

   a. In what areas of life are you diligent and focused? In what areas of life are you coasting, living unfocused?

   b. What's God saying to you here?

6. Read Revelation 22:1–5 and consider again the reality of Christ's kingdom and how superior it is to any earthly ambition or endeavor. I'd rather be a doorkeeper in the house of my God than a princess anywhere else. Spend some time with the Lord, asking Him to stir up in you a fresh passion for His Word and a tenacious faith to carry out His work.

7. Here's an assignment for you: Ask the Lord to show you an inheritance verse for your next place of promise. Study it, memorize it, and hang on to it. God's Word is a powerful weapon in your hand and on your tongue!

⤳ DISCUSSION STARTERS ⤳

1. It's interesting how we tend to take credit for our strengths and judge others for being weak in that same area, when in reality God makes us strong in particular areas so we can help those who are weak. How has God worked through one of your strengths to help someone who's weak in that same area (finances, fitness, organization, etc.)?

2. Do you feel tempted at times to take credit for and feel superior about your strengths? What do you do with those feelings?

3. How does criticism affect you? How about mean-spirited people? What do you do to get back to a place of peace and perspective again?

4. If you had to come up with a tag line to define God's beautiful purpose for your life, what would it be? This may take some work and several conversations with friends who know you well (e.g., my friend Kay recently realized that her tag line is "Heal the Church, So We Can Heal the World." This helps her understand why she's more drawn to soul-care type ministries than being a greeter at church).

5. Envision yourself at the end of your life. For what do you want people to remember you? What would finishing strong look like to you?

Acknowledgments

To these dear friends, colleagues, and family members, I offer up my most sincere, heartfelt thanks:

Mary DeMuth, whose literary expertise is a heaven-sent gift. Thank you, Mary, for your friendship, insight, and direction. You've helped shape my message, made it surer, clearer, and more concise. I love you, friend.

Jeff Braun (and the whole Bethany House Publishers team), whose heart for Jesus shines bright and strong. Thank you for so earnestly believing in this project and for so graciously welcoming me to the BHP family. It's an honor to serve alongside you.

Literary agent Steve Laube, who helped me to take this message from my heart and put it on the printed page. Thank you for stepping in and for standing with me. I look forward to what God has in store in the years ahead!

Naomi Duncan for not only being a tremendous booking agent, but for being an even truer friend. You *get me,* and that means the world to me. I've absolutely loved partnering with you and have been so grateful for the years we worked together. I'll miss you! Thank you. For everything.

Dick Whitworth for being a godly, strong, and hilarious leader. Truly, you're the best boss I've ever had. I love coming to the station every day, and I look forward to seeing God move even more mightily in the days to come through Faith Radio! Thank you for believing in me, for giving me the flexibility and freedom to write and speak to women, and for wisely seeing how these pieces all fit divinely together. Thank you, Dick. I appreciate you more than words can say.

Neil Stavem for being a Christ-follower first and a program director second; it's an honor to serve with you. And though you act like a curmudgeon on occasion, I know that underneath it all you're a tenderhearted guy with a great sense of humor. Bless you for your amazing support and leadership. I'm still chuckling over your suggested title for the book: *Buck Up, Buttercup.* It fits, but not really. But it's really funny.

Don Rupp, for always being there at the right time in my moments of grief. You're a radio icon, but even more significant, you're a man of God. Thank you for your friendship.

To the rest of my co-workers at KTIS: Dr. Virts, Jason, Keith, Morgan, Scott, Elizabeth, Tim, Grace, Theresa, Jen, Cheri, Kathy, Lisa, Pam, David, Dave, Matt, Ted, PK, Kay, Julene, Jeanne, Nicole, Sara, Eric, Gully, Mark, Justin, Carl, Dan, Sue, Rich, and Joyce. I love you all!

My sample readers: Daryl Jackson, Lynn Ferguson, Bonnie Newberg, Kathy Schwanke, Kay Blake, Karen Telle, Lisa Irwin, Patty Larson, Barb Odom, Sherri Reynertson-Zimmerman, Cindy Larson, Susan Stuart, Stephanie Johnson, Patty Fischer, Barbie Schmalzer, Peg Kohler, and Kristen Larson. Thank you for working through these chapters as I wrote them. I love your heart for the Lord, your heart for the women who'll read this book, and your heart for me. Couldn't do this without you. Love you to pieces!

My intercessors for standing on the wall for me when I'm out on the road, for praying me through my grief process while writing this book, and for investing in the lives of women you'll never meet this side of heaven. May God give you glimpses of your future reward. You're all heroes in my book (and in His).

Jake Larson, Luke and Kristen Larson, Jordan and Anita Larson, for being wonderful children, beautiful human beings, and treasured friends. Dad and I love praying for you as you walk out God's purposes for you. We're so proud to claim you as our own. Thanks for listening to me read over the phone. I smile when I think of it. Love you so.

Kevin Larson for being the love of my life, my greatest support, and an amazing partner in ministry. You're goofy, strong, steadfast, and patient: a perfect mix for me. May we continue to believe God for the impossible; may we—through Christ—leave no stone unturned, live without regret, and accomplish every purpose God had in mind for us before time began. When He looks to us, may He find faith in us. I love you, honey.

My precious Jesus, thank You for saving my soul, healing my hurts, and making something out of nothing. I marvel every day when I think of Your love and Your redemptive purposes.

Lord Jesus,

I offer up this book to You. Take this small sacrifice into Your beautiful, scarred hands, breathe divine life into these words, that they may nourish, heal, and mobilize an army of holy confident, humbly dependent women. It's in Your hands to make great. May You perform a miracle in the heart of every woman who picks up this book. I love You more with each new day. Amen.

Notes

Epigraph

1. Bruce Wilkinson, *The Dream Giver* (Sisters, OR: Multnomah Books, 2003), front flap.

Introduction: Do You Believe You're Called?

1. L. B. Cowman, *Streams in the Desert* (Grand Rapids, MI: Zondervan, 1997), 125.
2. *Oxford American Writer's Thesaurus,* www.oxfordreference.com.
3. Chip Ingram, *Holy Ambition* (Chicago: Moody Publishers, 2010), 12.

Chapter 1: Believe You're Called

1. Matthew Barnett, *The Cause Within You* (Carol Stream, IL: BarnaBooks, 2011), 41.
2. Warren Wiersbe, *The Wiersbe Bible Commentary* (Colorado Springs: David C. Cook, 2007), 43.
3. Ibid.

Chapter 2: Love *Your* Story

1. Edythe Draper, ed., *Draper's Book of Quotations for the Christian World* (Wheaton, IL: Tyndale House, 1992), 177, #3215.
2. Ann Voskamp, *One Thousand Gifts* (Grand Rapids, MI: Zondervan, 2010), 113.
3. Ibid., 135.

Chapter 3: Wait on God

1. David Timms, *Sacred Waiting* (Bloomington, MN: Bethany House Publishers, 2009), 21.
2. Susie Larson, story adapted from *Embracing Your Freedom* (Chicago: Moody Publishers, 2009), 178–181.

3. Samuel Dickey Gordon in *Streams in the Desert* (Grand Rapids, MI: Zondervan, 1997), 313.

Chapter 4: Face Your Fears

1. A. W. Tozer, *I Talk Back to the Devil* (Camp Hill, PA: Wing Spread Publishers, 1990), 4.
2. Eric Ludy, *Wrestling Prayer* (Eugene, OR: Harvest House Publishers, 2009), 80.

Chapter 5: Discern Your Preparation

1. L. B. Cowman, *Streams in the Desert* (Grand Rapids, MI: Zondervan, 1997), 191.
2. William MacDonald coined this phrase, as found in *Believer's Bible Commentary* (Nashville: Thomas Nelson, 1995), 73.
3. MacDonald, *Believer's Bible Commentary*, 1933.

Chapter 6: Silence Your Enemy

1. A. W. Tozer, *I Talk Back to the Devil* (Camp Hill, PA: Wing Spread Publishers, 2008), 15.
2. William MacDonald, *Believer's Bible Commentary* (Nashville: Thomas Nelson, 1995), 1708 (emphasis mine).
3. Jim Cymbala, *You Were Made for More* (Grand Rapids, MI: Zondervan, 2008), 208.
4. Warren Wiersbe, *The Wiersbe Bible Commentary* (Colorado Springs: David C. Cook, 2007), 991.
5. Learn about the weapons of our warfare by studying Ephesians 6.
6. W. N. Tomkins, "Christ's Grave Is Vacant Now," reprinted in *Believer's Bible Commentary*, 1708.

Chapter 7: Follow His Lead

1. Bruce Wilkinson, *Beyond Jabez* (Sisters, OR: Multnomah Books, 2005), 80.
2. The story of the wedding at Cana is found in the gospel of John, chapter 2.
3. Warren Wiersbe, *The Wiersbe Bible Commentary* (Colorado Springs: David C. Cook, 2007), 895.
4. Jim Cymbala, *You Were Made for More* (Grand Rapids, MI: Zondervan, 2008), 26.
5. Rick Renner, *Sparkling Gems From the Greek* (Tulsa, OK: Teach All Nations, 2007), 598.
6. Wilkinson, *Beyond Jabez*, 79.

Chapter 8: Engage Your Faith

1. A. B. Simpson in *Streams in the Desert* (Grand Rapids, MI: Zondervan, 1997), 165.
2. Jeff Olson, *The Slight Edge: Secret to a Successful Life* (Lake Dallas, TX: Momentum Media, 2005), my paraphrase of the book's overall message.
3. Selected reading, *Streams in the Desert* (Grand Rapids, MI: Zondervan, 1997), August 17 reading.

4. NIV study note, *Life in the Spirit Study Bible* (Grand Rapids, MI: Zondervan, 2003), 910.

Chapter 9: Find High Ground

1. Anne Graham Lotz, *Expecting to See Jesus* (Grand Rapids, MI: Zondervan, 2010), 57.
2. Ann Voskamp, *One Thousand Gifts* (Grand Rapids, MI: Zondervan, 2010), 177.

Chapter 10: Stay the Course

1. Nathaniel William Taylor in *Streams in the Desert* (Grand Rapids, MI: Zondervan, 1997), 416.
2. My imaginative portrayal of Jairus and the woman with the issue of blood as told in the gospel of Mark, chapter 5.
3. Mark Batterson, *The Circle Maker* (Grand Rapids, MI: Zondervan, 2011), 94.
4. George Body, *Joy and Strength* (New York: Barnes & Noble Books, 1993 edition), 274.
5. Warren Wiersbe, *The Wiersbe Bible Commentary* (Colorado Springs: David C. Cook, 2007), 42.

Chapter 11: Take New Land

1. A. B. Simpson in *Streams in the Desert* (Grand Rapids, MI: Zondervan, 1997), 429.

Chapter 12: Last Long, Finish Strong

1. Victor Hugo in *Streams in the Desert* (Grand Rapids, MI: Zondervan, 1997), 216.
2. Hetty Green and William Hearst stories adapted from *Warren Wiersbe's New Testament Bible Commentary* (Colorado Springs: David C. Cook, 2007), 584, 589.
3. Rick Joyner, *There Were Two Trees in the Garden* (Charlotte, NC: Morningstar Publications, 1992), 10.
4. NIV *Life in the Spirit Study Bible* (Grand Rapids, MI: Zondervan, 2003), 1477, emphasis mine.

Susie Larson is a radio host, author, national media voice for Moody Radio, and national speaker. She hosts the daily live talk show, *Live the Promise with Susie Larson*. Susie connects weekly with thousands of women through her radio program, devotional blog, and her daily faith questions on Facebook. Her passion is to see women everywhere strengthened in their faith and mobilized to live out their high calling in Jesus Christ.

Susie's previous books include *Growing Grateful Kids*, *Embracing Your Freedom*, *The Uncommon Woman*, *Alone in Marriage*, and *Balance That Works When Life Doesn't*. She has appeared on radio and TV programs across the country, including *Focus on the Family*, *FamilyLife Today*, *Moody Midday*, *LIFE Today*, and *The Harvest Show*.

Susie and her husband, Kevin, work alongside recording artist Sara Groves and her husband, Troy, with International Justice Mission as advocates for victims of human trafficking and slavery.

Susie and Kevin live near Minneapolis, Minnesota, and have three grown sons. For more information, visit www.susielarson.com.

Don't Miss the DVD Study Companion to *Your Beautiful Purpose*

Host a six-week small group study at home or at church—hassle free! Author Susie Larson herself can lead your study group with this DVD companion to *Your Beautiful Purpose*, freeing you from the daunting responsibility of leading *and* facilitating a group at the same time.

In 30-minute sessions that correlate with the book's six-week study guide, the DVD study companion includes
- the key teaching points of each book section
- extra content not covered in the book
- and introductions to the Discussion Starter questions at the end of each chapter